the GREATEST ENTREPRENEUR
in the WORLD

Also by Sean C. Castrina

8 Unbreakable Rules for Business Start-Up Success
8 Unbreakable Rules for Business Start-Up Success Workbook
The Greatest Entrepreneur in the World Workbook

The GREATEST ENTREPRENEUR *in the* WORLD

THE TALE OF 7 PILLARS
Surviving Startup to Becoming the Giant

SEAN C. CASTRINA

New York

the GREATEST ENTREPRENEUR *in the* WORLD
THE TALE OF 7 PILLARS
Surviving Startup to Becoming the Giant

Published in New York, New York, by Morgan James Publishing. Morgan James and The Entrepreneurial Publisher are trademarks of Morgan James, LLC. www.MorganJamesPublishing.com

The Morgan James Speakers Group can bring authors to your live event. For more information or to book an event visit The Morgan James Speakers Group at www.TheMorganJamesSpeakersGroup.com.

This book is a word of fiction. Names, characters, businesses, organizations, places and events and incidents either are the products of the author's imagination or are used fictitiously. Any resemblance to actual persons, living or dead, events, or locales is entirely coincidental.

ISBN 978-1-63047-610-6 paperback
ISBN 978-1-63047-611-3 eBook
ISBN 978-1-63047-612-0 audio
Library of Congress Control Number:
2015905163

A free eBook edition is available
with the purchase of this print book.

CLEARLY PRINT YOUR NAME ABOVE IN UPPER CASE
Instructions to claim your free eBook edition:
1. Download the BitLit app for Android or iOS
2. Write your name in **UPPER CASE** on the line
3. Use the BitLit app to submit a photo
4. Download your eBook to any device

Cover Design by:
Rachel Lopez
www.r2cdesign.com

Interior Design by:
Bonnie Bushman
The Whole Caboodle Graphic Design

In an effort to support local communities and raise awareness and funds, Morgan James Publishing donates a percentage of all book sales for the life of each book to Habitat for Humanity Peninsula and Greater Williamsburg

Get involved today, visit
www.MorganJamesBuilds.com

Habitat
for Humanity®
Peninsula and
Greater Williamsburg
Building Partner

TABLE OF CONTENTS

INTRODUCTION

Are you an entrepreneur? An affirmative answer to this question unlocks a life that most would agree is a wonderful one to participate in. There is no more of a revered list on Earth than *Forbes'* annual list of the wealthiest 400 Americans. With a combined net worth in the trillions, no one on this mount Rushmore of wealth dare apply with anything short of a 10-figure treasure chest. Within just a few years, the bar will surely be 11 figures.

There was a time when children wanted to grow up to be a doctors, lawyers, policemen or teachers, but now more than ever, a successful entrepreneur is the crown jewel of careers. It is the only one where the greater the achievement, the more freedom you have and less you actually have to do that you don't want to. Oh, what a freedom entrepreneurial success provides, but not so with the aforementioned fields, where being the most accomplished requires no less than a 70-hour workweek and still having to answer to a boss. And let's not forget, you can still get fired or downsized no matter how loyal you have been. Not so with the entrepreneur, who creates jobs and the wealth that keeps a country's economy moving.

"What is an entrepreneur?" and, "How can I be one?" are questions that get asked too often with no clear answer. For one, an entrepreneur is someone with the gift to start something that provides a profit that currently does not exist. That is *my* definition; so don't bother comparing it to the one listed in Webster's Dictionary. I want to quickly define profit because I do believe it goes far broader than a dollar. Do you have an idea that could provide shoes for those who cannot afford them? That sure would be profitable to the person who does not have them so please go forth and be a successful entrepreneur. Do you work for a company that needs to grow and you have a few thoughts that could birth new profit from within? Then go forth and present your plan of attack (with a few warnings, I could share on how to have these ideas benefit you personally as well).

I have started more businesses than I have fingers and soon more than I have toes (not to mention digesting more than 200 books on every subject related to starting and growing a business). I am convinced I have discovered a few pillars, as I call them, that must be established to first survive (because there will be a season when survival is all you can hope for) and, finally, to help your company, division or organization become a giant (and reap the spoils that status brings).

So the answer I share is: Yes, you can be an entrepreneur because it is a learned skill. I confess, it will come easier to some than others, but we have all been taught at some time or another that anything worth getting requires work and sacrifice. Being a successful entrepreneur is no different, but what is different is the payoff. I would argue no field offers greater rewards than that of an accomplished entrepreneur. In this book, I aim to paint a picture of what those rewards can look like while teaching the pillars that I've learned to survive startup and become the giant.

Chapter 1

MY DECISION

A s I look out the window of my office on the 28th floor of the old Illinois Bell Building, I feel as if I am looking out of a fish tank. My name is Johnny Dawkins. This building was once occupied by a former retail titan known the world over, but now we own it in a partnership and occupy 14 floors mortared between AB Investment Group who sits above us and Global Information Security. What keeps me humble is that both companies I just mentioned were not even in existence a decade ago. This esteemed building became available a decade ago during the very public collapse of a retail- and catalog-pioneering giant who never transitioned into the information age. Inside these walls of glass and steel it is quiet and still, but outside on the city streets there is constant motion and noise.

The city of Chicago is abuzz with life. Businesswomen and businessmen hustle down the sidewalks toward their offices, hardhat workers operate heavy equipment as they build the city's next skyscraper, arteries of traffic wind way too slowly for anyone's taste; all are swarming around this massive concrete forest of architecture called the Windy City. Yet, I stand above this scene, in total silence, watching from my office.

Whatever thickness my window glass is, it is enough to cancel out an entire metropolis of noise. From my glassed perch, I can look through those floor-to-ceiling windows in near every direction. I have a one hundred and eighty degree view of Chicago, my hometown. Most of the time, I catch myself looking north in the direction of where I grew up: my old neighborhood of Wrigleyville. Wrigleyville is the name of the area surrounding Wrigley field, home of the Cubs and the place of many boyhood memories of roaring times on hot summer days. I lived about three blocks from the stadium on Addison Street in a working-class neighborhood. I don't live there now, but I like to think about it and reminisce. A little farther north is where I went to college at Northwestern University in Evanston, Illinois. The school is located along the handsome shoreline of Lake Michigan.

The clock on my office wall reads 2:02 p.m. He's two minutes late. Maybe traffic, I think, and turn to a picture of my wife, Christine, on my desk. I can hear her voice urging me to finally retire my position in the company, encouraging me to select my replacement today. She knows a new passion has arisen within me, actually it has arisen in both of us and that is why it excites me so. I was a founding partner of what has grown from a single newspaper to what now is MW Media, a global media organization. Even I am struck by our growth and current position as an influential and profitable empire. I am very proud of my life's work, but the past year I have had a desire that has nothing to do with business. The desire has taken me captive.

At 64, with enough money to last a few lifetimes, I feel the desire—in fact, the need—to apply my gifts to organize, to motivate, and to achieve in something other than business. That desire even feels foreign to me, as I think I have spent nearly 35 years focused on profit, personal net worth, and our companies' stock prices. I now want a life spending more time with Christine, our children and their young children. I step quietly across the office floor whispering to myself. "I may be leaving. I may not be in this office anymore." That thought alone startles me out of my gaze across the concrete landscape.

Suddenly Linda, my personal secretary of more than two decades, announces the arrival of Charlie Calloway. Charlie had been the youngest executive producer at CCN and he presently holds the position of vice president of TSS, the largest satellite television company pioneering new platforms in the expanding world of media. Charlie, at 48, is looking to make that final move up, and becoming president of MW Media would be the move of a lifetime.

Within seven days, I am requested though not formally required to finalize and then recommend a replacement for myself to the board. With a new acting president and CEO in place, I am to sit back as founder and still largest individual shareholder and just let someone else lead a company that I birthed into existence more than 30 years ago. Someone like Charlie Calloway perhaps. Charlie is the top choice of the Board of Directors. They have been charmed by his steady manner, impressed with his credentials, and persuaded by his modern ideas. A Wharton business school graduate with a pedigree everyone on Wall Street would view as a great hire for our continued transition into the new global market. Sounds great, right? Then why doesn't it feel right?

Our business is media; from the endangered print magazines and newspaper holdings, which I am still partial to, to cable television and, just recently, satellite broadcasting. The industry has many guidelines and regulations; it also requires a sensibility that few can grasp, not to mention a need for understanding all mediums of journalism and entertainment, not to mention advertising, still our largest source of revenue, with subscriptions a close second. Charlie is qualified with his degrees and status, but is he really the right person for the job? Is he fit to shepherd our more than 3,600 employees as well as a battalion of contract workers?

THE INTERVIEW

Charlie and I have met several times in the past six months, so when he enters the office he shakes my hand. His grip is always firm, as if he has practiced this simple gesture countless times preparing for moments such as this. His appearance is impeccable, wrapped in a custom suit with a shirt, tie and handkerchief that I know someone set out for him. I don't blame him for this. Appearance does matter, even if we all would like to think it doesn't. He has the smile of an evening

TV news anchor, one that is completely disarming. With the usual pleasantries out of the way, he immediately begins presenting me with a passionate closing sales pitch explaining why he should garner my support to lead the company. His presentation style begins to mirror a closing argument meant to sway an undecided jury. Despite his supreme confidence, I believe he knew within that I had not yet been sold.

He leads using only my first name, Johnny. He has addressed me as Johnny from day one and I am still not certain why. At my age, a "Mr. Dawkins" in our initial meetings would have been protocol, but that is his style—disarming anyone in the room. His people skills are enviable.

"I have some thoughts on how we should grow our global position," he says. From that opening statement, most of what comes next is a blur. He understands the global market as well as anybody and sticks to the arena he knows best.

I interject to ask his plans for our U.S. position and older holdings such as print and radio, which he embraces the same way one does their mother-in-law after the I do's— saying enough to be a part of the family but not enough to get in trouble.

That is the part that has bothered me. He answers everything perfect and safe. I would be open to a debate on our approach and would even welcome differing strategies, but he has chosen to take the position that his resume is enough to get this job, possibly even thinking we should feel lucky to have him after our recent public embarrassment with my last would-be successor. I'll save that for later.

His whole speech is one I have heard more than once and not just from him, as the board echoes his vision. He is affable, educated, and quite persuasive. In fact, I have interviewed only lesser candidates over the previous months without much hope of hire. Charlie completes his monologue describing the goals he has for the first year of doing my job and how he would manage and even improve things.

I must say I am impressed, but not convinced. Why? I question myself. I have to admit the man knows his game. He has a few fresh ideas and he talks about them without using empty buzzwords. He is in tune with new technology and he seems to have the right experience. Surely, I have to concede that Charlie Calloway is a very good candidate to take over for me.

After nearly 40 minutes of listening, I break my silence. "Well Charlie, you seem well qualified. I'm sure you would…" At this point, I utter words that seem canned as I hear them come from my mouth, but I try to smile in a way that I can only hope makes them seem genuine.

I inform him that I will be meeting with the board soon to make my final recommendation, and I tell him I appreciated the opportunity to meet with him over the last few months and wished him well no matter what the outcome is, assuring him continued success will surely be in his future. He thanks me for my encouraging words as I escort him to our main lobby where I watch him leave. I was wanting—and if I can be honest, praying—for a sign that would confirm to me he was the correct choice.

As I return to my office, the phone rings. Jake Worthington, our senior board member and chairman, is ready for the news as if there was a firm delivery date for a child and I was to inform him of the specifics. Jake made his money the hard way, as he has reminded me countless times, as if there is an easy way to make money. His fortune initially came from billboards on highways, then in every other place you could possible put one. For that, I have to give him credit for creativity because I never would have thought there was just short of a billion dollars in it, but somehow this pit bull had figured out a way to extract a fortune with this simple business idea.

Jake meets me with his usual bombastic tone. "Is he our guy? Oh, don't give me *no*, Johnny." Interrupting Worthington is like stepping in front of a steam engine, so I let him finish. "The board loves and appreciates you, but this speculation over you leaving has our stockholders wanting this transition to be smooth. We need to hire a winner."

This speech I have heard often lately reiterating the need for the "big hire." Though I am not sure I agree.

"Our interview was very profitable," I assure him, "and I will have my recommendation to the board by the close of next week." I remind him that much of the mess we are in and our need for the so-called big hire was because the board fell in love with a fickle mistress and I would not let that mistake dictate another foolish rush to appoint someone who we would come to regret.

This interruption on my part, delivering the painful truth, slows Jake's usual confidence. I hear him take a breath that says,

"I know you're right, but please let's get this done," though he doesn't utter a single word.

I like Jake and remove him from this painful hook he is on, assuring him that I also want a smooth transition as well and will make my decision within days. Though at this moment, I'm not sure what I will be delivering to him.

When I hang up the phone, I start looking east from my office window through the clouds, remembering a smaller, quieter town that made you think it was way out there in the middle of the country, when in reality, it was only a little more than an hour away. I'm looking in the direction of the town of Daytonville. I begin to remember a phone ringing nearly 40-years ago.

Chapter 2

THE CALL

I could hear the familiar sound of ringing as I held the phone to my ear waiting for someone to answer. It was summer and quite warm, an oppressive heat, in the old familiar press office of *The Daytonville Herald*. Our large windows were propped open, begging for air to enter with the assistance of industrial fans large enough to propel the liftoff of a plane. They blew endlessly while coworkers hustled past me.

It was in my second summer following graduation from Northwestern, where I played baseball on scholarship and received a degree in journalism. I had taken the job at the *Herald* because they assured me they would give me the chance to write my own stories unlike the opportunities at the larger papers where I would effectively be an understudy for who knows how long.

After a few rings, a man's voice answered, "Hello, Advanced Window Cleaning, how may I help you today?"

"Good afternoon, I would like to speak with Mr. Emmit Lake please. I am with *The Daytonville Herald*, and we would like to interview Mr. Lake about an award Advanced Window Cleaning has won." Advanced Window Cleaning was a residential and commercial glass cleaning company that predominantly served commercial retail clients as well as large government buildings throughout the state of Indiana.

"Which award is that?" asked the voice.

"The Excellence in Service award," I told him. "And I see this is not the first time the company has won the award."

"Well… ahhh, I wouldn't mind having a story that gives my team some credit and recognition. They're a great group."

"Mr. Lake?" I asked.

"Yes," replied the voice.

"Mr. Lake, is that you?"

"That's correct," Mr. Lake assured me.

Caught off guard, I began to stammer a bit. "I'm surprised. I… I didn't expect to speak with you directly though I had hoped I might, sir. I thought I'd reach your receptionist or secretary."

"Nothing like first-hand information," Emmit Lake calmly offered. "This is how I check in with my customers and get a pulse on my companies."

"Interesting. How does that work?" I found myself asking.

Mr. Lake answered, "Well, if you really want to know, I field random calls late in the day from each of my various businesses. I ask each caller how they heard about my company and then I listen very carefully because the answers to this one question are key to the health of my businesses."

"You personally field calls every day for each of your businesses?"

"Well," Lake considered the question. "I give each company a bit of a physical exam by taking about ten calls a month for each."

"How does that help?" I asked. "I mean, what can you tell from ten phone calls a month?"

He openly shared, answering as if this was not the first time the question had been asked. "Well, after I ask a caller how they heard about our company, I like to hear three or four of them say they are new customers; without new customers, you cannot grow. I want three or four callers to say they have been our customers and are using our company again, because repeat customers let you know your company is fulfilling its promises. Additionally, I hope three or four will be referrals. Referrals are the result of exceeding expectations of existing customers to the point they become passionate enough to tell others about the business. If the answers during these calls are not happening with this approximate ratio, something may be off, and the company may require more attention or need a change."

As I stood in the office of *The Daytonville Herald*, I became aware that the interview had already begun. I grabbed a pencil from the desk beside me. I scribbled down note after note as he spoke. I soon realized, this wasn't any interview, he was telling me his business method! Remembering the reason I called him, I said, "I sure would appreciate an interview, Mr. Lake. It would be valuable to hear more of your business ideas … and we'd be happy to give your team some well-deserved credit."

"Okay, why don't we meet Thursday at Sarah's Diner at say, 12:45, and as much as I have enjoyed our conversation I do not believe I got your name."

"Sorry, my name is Johnny Dawkins, and I am an assistant editor here at the *Herald*. Thursday, 12:45 at Sara's is perfect. Thank you, sir." Just as I placed the phone's receiver in its cradle, the senior editor of the paper tapped me on the shoulder. His name was William Kennedy Kincade III, but everyone called him Billy.

BILLY KINCADE

"Don't tell me that was Emmit Lake!" Billy stood as tall as he was wide, always wearing suspenders with a bow tie to showcase his presence. Calling him a character of sorts is an understatement. Holding his familiar mug of coffee in one hand and a near-finished cigarette in the other, he had an annoying habit of constantly sniffing, as if he had an allergy of some sort, or was just too lazy to blow his nose.

"As a matter of fact," I told Billy, "it was. I'll be interviewing him on Thursday." Billy shook his head left-to-right for his usual dramatic affect. I often found him to be trenchant by nature.

"I've tried to get interviews with him over the years with little success, but he's always had a polite reason for not doing it. He's not much for personal publicity." Billy began to turn a bit red in the face. "If you're going to do this interview, you need to know a little background on the man.

"I understand you didn't grow up here like the rest of us, Johnny, but between all of his businesses, Emmit Lake employs a lot of locals. His worksite-cleanup company, Advanced Industrial, employed more than 500 people in the surrounding counties and did work in nearly every major city in the Midwest before he sold it. But his companies are not the type you find on the stock exchange."

Billy lowered his voice as if he was imparting delicate secrets. "No, Lake layers his holdings by starting one new business after another. Listen Johnny, in my research, I found more than a dozen local businesses he is responsible for, and I'm not convinced I'm even close to the number of businesses he actually owns in this region. It seems he started his career with a floor cleaning company, but people joke he has never had to fix, clean or shovel anything in over 30 years."

Billy leaned awkwardly close to my face. "Service companies were just the beginning. He used them to build a real estate portfolio anyone would envy. The story goes that his father and his family lost everything in the Great Depression, and as you can imagine it left a mark on him."

"Billy, don't get too excited. I think we may just be getting a cup of coffee together," I clarified. "Mr. Lake set the meeting time at 12:45 p.m. I sense it might only be a fifteen-minute interview and you're welcome to come."

THE GREATEST ENTREPRENEUR WE'D EVER KNOWN

Billy visibly struggled as he conceded, "No, no, that's all right. You landed the interview. You deserve it. He must have taken a liking to you. I've always wanted to open my own little business one day," he confided to me.

I wasn't even sure if Billy knew the last thought was audible, but he continued on with a random declaration. "Emmit Lake is the greatest entrepreneur Daytonville has ever known."

Billy was near retirement then, but I couldn't help but draw the conclusion that if Billy had interviewed Emmit earlier on, he would have learned how to accomplish his hidden dream.

Considering the grandness of his statement, he tempered it somewhat. "Maybe he's not great in the way J. Paul Getty, Andrew Carnegie or Henry Ford were great. He did not have that one great idea that became a fortune. He starts one business that leads to another, then he partners in a complementary business that brings him to buying the land or building that the company operates from. Then he repeats the model over and over. I have spoken with his partners and employees over the years—not on record, of course, just in conversations. They all say he has a "Pied Piper" effect that makes others want to join him on his ventures. He makes it look easy; makes you wonder why we aren't all doing it and I haven't even mentioned his charitable work, which is just as impressive as the businesses achievements."

"Sounds like a guy I can't wait to meet," I said.

But what I had secretly started wondering is what our paper would have looked like if someone like Emmit Lake owned it. All we heard since my first day at the paper is how unprofitable the paper was. We were constantly worried that a larger paper would absorb us one day. When that day happened, we feared the big paper wouldn't want the local stories. It was obvious at the time that the larger paper had a cookie cutter approach of running the same national and world stories with a faint trace of local stories when needed.

I remembered fondly what a simple Sunday paper provided for my family growing up. My mom retrieving coupons, my dad informing all of us at the dinner table of the world's events, and me fascinated by the sports page where I was introduced to my heroes with tales of their latest feats. Though I was fairly new to the industry, I saw worth in a local newspaper and believed small community news stories were the key to providing additional appreciated content that local advertisers would value.

A BRIEF HISTORY LESSON

The town of Daytonville was not what you would consider a small town but not large enough to be mentioned in the same breath with Chicago or Springfield. For years, Daytonville was a much-envied city as it once featured two substantial businesses that provided a large number of jobs to the community. One was American Mattresses and the other was Smith Anderson Insurance. It seems odd—almost out of place—that a settlement like Daytonville could birth an insurance company that almost everybody in America knows, in addition to a mattress company that supplies beds for the guests of nearly every motel in the country.

The insurance company had been around since the mid-1800s when it began protecting local farms and farmers from drought and loss. The mattress manufacturer emerged by making horse-drawn carriages equipped with padded seats and sturdy springs to absorb the jolts of the road. Producing padded seats eventually led to manufacturing mattresses, and this product would become the sole focus of the company by the early 1900s.

The town was quite fortunate by most standards to have two industries within its borders for a generation, but eventually its economy struggled when these two stalwarts of our community moved to Chicago and Indianapolis. This is why Emmit Lake's loyalty to the community by choosing to never relocate any of his ventures was so admired. Even the sale of Advanced Industrial, which became a much sought after company, carried a clause in the sales agreement calling for the main office to reside within 30 miles of Daytonville for a period of no less than 50 years from the sale date. And maybe more important was fact that Emmit sold Advanced to a former employee who became a partner in the business after years of loyal commitment as a field manager. Most of the people in town knew Emmit could have sold to outsiders, and for much more, but it was those choices that reflected his priorities and made him unique.

In my brief time reporting the news at the *Herald* those two years, I had the privilege of hearing many stories about the mattress company and the insurance company. I'd been told how, with nothing more than an idea about a cushion in a carriage, you could turn a small business into a national mattress mogul. To this day, I am still fascinated by the moment when a hunch brings forth a business that changes an entire town, an entire industry or even the world.

Chapter 3

THE MEETING

I remember it so vividly. Over the years, I have shared pieces of this story; always feeling the need to embellish its characters and events because they come off as benign and even simple, when in fact, they were life changing. The story has had layers spanning nearly 40 years to feature its full presentation and value.

I arrived on time at Sara's knowing it would be rude to be one minute late for such a sought-after interview. With its white brick exterior, Sara's was a well-known eatery that served as a popular lunch haven for office workers. It was just two blocks over from the *Herald* and one block from our municipal building. As I opened the door, I noticed an older gentleman waiting patiently by the hostess podium. He was meticulously groomed and sat with an upright posture that displayed confidence. He was wearing clothes that appeared both casual and professional, like it would be appropriate for either the golf course or for a board meeting. Was this Emmit? For some reason, my mind already assumed it was. He looked just how I pictured him.

"Mr. Lake?" I asked. The distinguished looking fellow with an even balance of grey dividing his once blond hair looked up, and we made eye contact. He gave me a warm smile while he tucked a white card in his pocket and stood up. Most people would dismiss the white card he put in his pocket, but I was a journalist. It was my job to notice details. He stepped forward, reached out his right hand, and grasped my shoulder firmly with his left hand.

"Hello, Johnny. Call me Emmit and thank you for joining me today." Emmit seemed so familiar and friendly I almost wondered if we'd met before. I immediately took a deep breath and relaxed a bit as his very nature disarmed me from the onset.

"Hello, nice to meet you. I hope I'm not late." I was worried he might have been waiting for me to arrive.

Emmit kindly waved off my apology. "Not at all. You are right on time. I decided years ago to be five minutes early for all my meetings. I don't like lateness. It shows disrespect to all parties involved. In fact, I never hire someone who is late for a job interview."

Emmit looked me in the eye. "Not ever. If they aren't trying to impress you before they get the job, they never will after you give it to them."

You never hire someone who is late. I later realized this was one of countless axioms shared at this lunch. He doled out maxims like seeds planted by a farmer, and you could tell he shared his words as if he hoped the listener would use them.

I can remember the air conditioner and its loud humming in that old diner that day and how refreshing it was to escape the July heat. I recall the sound of the cooks working in the kitchen and the smell of coffee in the air. I also recollect the way Emmit spoke to the hostess with such familiarity,

"Hello Margaret, so nice to see you today. What a beautiful day outside." It was clear then to me he was used to the heat, as temperatures that are close to 100 degrees were not what I would call beautiful so maybe he just viewed near everything in a positive frame. At first, with the way he spoke to the hostess, I thought perhaps she had served him before as he displayed a genuine interest in what she was sharing. Emmit would later reveal how he simply read Margaret's nametag when she turned to take us to our seats.

"Yes sir, warmer than I'm used to, but I like it," Margaret commented with a light New England accent.

"Where are you from?" Emmit asked. He made eye contact and there was a sincerity in his tone that actually made you think he was genuinely interested in her reply. "You must be fairly new here."

Margaret, attractive in a simple way, with pale skin and the kindest smile, spoke with minimal expression in her eyes; distant and distracted. I later realized she was homesick. "Portland, Maine. Lot colder up there," she said. "Just graduated from high school and I needed to come down here to help take care of my grandma. I hope to take some college classes while I'm here."

Margaret caught herself and shook her head as if to wake herself up. "Sorry. You don't want to hear about all that, sir."

Emmit quickly put the young woman at ease. "You must be Ida Lewis's grandchild! I was told she had a smart and lovely young lady from Maine coming to stay with her. Well, my word, and here you are. I'm going to give you my business card. If you or your grandmother, need anything at all, you just give my office a call. Promise?"

"Okay, I promise," Margaret muttered, looking down at the business card in her hand. Watching, I sensed an intrinsic good in Emmitt—a genuine likeability.

"And put my name down as a referral when you apply for the local college once you're ready to get back to school. If you have any trouble there, you just let me know."

"Thank you, sir."

"No, thank you Margaret, you gave us the best seat in the house. I think you're going to make a fine hostess here." I noticed the diner's seats were pretty much all the same, but Margaret smiled to herself and drifted away looking at the business card in her hand as if she'd found a golden ticket.

Emmit and I read our menus and considered our lunch options. As we simultaneously placed our menus on the table, I opened our dialogue.

"Twelve forty-five is an interesting time to meet, and I'm going to venture a guess there is a reason you chose this particular time."

Emmit grinned a bit as if he had found something that was lost in a drawer. "Years ago, I began setting all of my meetings at quarter 'til."

"Quarter 'til?"

"Yes, Johnny, you see," Emmit leaned toward me a little, "when I meet folks on the hour, they assume they will receive a full hour of my time. If I start my meetings at quarter 'til, people arrive prepared for only fifteen minutes and they generally regard any additional time as a courtesy that I am granting."

"Oh…" I think back to my own reaction to the specific time of choice. "That's true."

I glanced at my watch nervously, but Emmit reassured me. "Not to worry, son, I've set aside plenty of time for you today."

Our waitress, with a nametag that read "Misty" arrived. She was as plump as she was cheerful. "Well look who's here: Mr. Lake! How are you today, sir? So nice to see you! Sweet tea as usual?"

Emmit and Misty shared a smile. "Sure, Misty, thank you. Misty, this is Johnny Dawkins. Johnny works with *The Daytonville Herald.*"

"Hello," I said politely, but Misty had some grievances to air.

"You work for the *Herald?*"

"Uh, yes ma'am."

"Well, uh…" Misty sneered at me, "y'all need to start getting the weather right. My daddy's field is dying without water. Last week you said it was going to rain, two times you said it. So, where's the rain? He ain't had a drop."

I began to apologize, but Misty cut me off. "Y'all just need to start getting it right."

"Yes ma'am. We'll try harder."

"All right then. What do you want to drink, honey?" Misty smiled broadly at me.

"Sweet tea, please."

I noticed Emmit smiling and nodding his head ever so slightly as Misty sauntered away to get our drinks.

Some time later, he asked me if I remembered that exchange with Misty. When I said yes, he told me it was that very moment watching me handle her sass with grace and humility that he decided right there that he liked me. And that simple discovery would lead to years of generosity with his time and teaching leading up to and beyond what would later become my destiny.

My moment to impress didn't come a moment too soon as I turned to Emmit after Misty left and made my pitch for a bigger story. "My assignment for the *Herald* was a story recognizing your companies' achievements and announcing the award—and I still plan to, as you said it was your intention to reward your team for work well done. I would appreciate the opportunity to interview some of your key staff, but to be honest, I find myself most fascinated with how someone becomes a business owner and a successful one. Without that, there would be no story because there would be no business to give an award to."

"You're very perceptive, Johnny. But I sense there is a bigger story you are interested in today. Is that right?" I looked down at my prepared questions and indeed he was correct. Billy ignited a curiosity in me that I had to have explained.

"Yes," I admitted. "See, rumor has it in town—and I have this on good authority—that you are the greatest entrepreneur this area has ever known. These are other people's words, not mine."

Emmit gave a hearty chuckle. "That surely is a bit exaggerated, but I would like to think I know a few things that allow me to bring an idea that fulfills a need or meets a strong want to profitability. In fact, that is all I set out to do in business."

I decided the time was right to begin my quest launching into my first question. "Emmit," I started, but I quickly confessed to him that I felt more conformable calling him sir or Mr. Lake. I was guessing his age to be mid-50s, although he had energy and wit to envy. He assured me that Emmit was fine—and, in fact, his preference.

And so it began. "How did you first begin your entrepreneurial journey?"

"When I was about 11 or 12 years old." Emmit replied without hesitation.

"Wow! That's pretty young," I admitted.

"It was a lemonade stand." He started to laugh, then let me in on the joke. "Ok, it started with a lemonade stand, but we quickly added popcorn because we learned it just makes you even more thirsty."

"That makes sense." I laughed with him, then wondered out loud, "Does owning a lemonade stand make you an entrepreneur?"

ENTREPRENEURSHIP 101

"It sure does! See, an entrepreneur is someone who initiates any enterprise knowing that success is not guaranteed. But this person does know that if success is achieved, there will be a payoff equal to or hopefully far greater than any risk or time they have invested. People act as entrepreneurs more often than they realize. When you take full responsibility for a goal—or project for that matter—you've really got to think for yourself and find a way to make an effective plan in order to accomplish what you've set out to accomplish. That's what an entrepreneur does. My best friend Mark and I didn't know we were entrepreneurs when we sold lemonade and soon popcorn on hot summer days over 40 years ago, but we were. That's all it takes. Recognize something people need or want, then find a way to give it to them. If you're smart you find other things they want or need— that is the mission—at a price that is both fair to the customer and profitable for you. That's business in its simplest form."

Chapter 4

THE FIRST PILLAR

Misty brings out our tea, which gave me a moment to process what Emmit said entrepreneurship really was.

"Thank you, Misty." Emmit looked up at the waitress. "I'll have the chicken salad sandwich please."

"I'll have the same, please," I chimed in. Misty scribbled down our orders on her pad and was gone as quickly as she appeared.

"So why did you want to start a business?" I asked. "You were just a kid."

Emmit turned back to me. "We wanted baseball cards. Our goal, though I am sure we did not call it a goal back then, was to make enough money to buy a few packs of baseball cards. We enjoyed selling and trading them. Kids at school

25

would pay what little they might have had in those days for the right cards, and it was always fun to show off your collection. That was enough motivation for Mark and me to weather the heat when all our pals were swimming at the lake and just having fun."

I asked Emmit how the business fared and his face lit up as he remembered.

"We had a great plan. Mark had the notion to set our stand up at his house, because he lived on the corner of two streets and therefore more traffic would see us. Location. Location. Location. I had the idea of hollering out 'HOMEMADE LEMONADE! GET YOUR ICE-COLD, REFRESHING HOMEMADE LEMONADE HERE!' I was like a sideshow barker at a carnival."

Emmit paused a moment to squeeze a slice of lemon into his iced tea and take a sip. "In hindsight," Emmit continued, "I was sharing with the marketplace what our products advantages were: 'ice cold' and 'homemade.' The popcorn with its great smell did its own attracting so I didn't even need to mention that. In looking back, you could say it was my first marketing campaign. Mark delivered what he could to our little business—a first-rate location, table and a popcorn machine from an old theater that went under in nearby Jessup where his father had done work. I provided ice, some lemons, sugar, a well-crafted sign, and a loud voice, not to mention the idea to do it in the first place. I have to say I have repeated this formula of partnering countless times and with tremendous results: bringing someone to the business who offered something I could not provide. Before long, Mark and I had enough pocket money to buy all the cards we wanted. We were not just entrepreneurs, we were *successful* entrepreneurs."

"At only 12-years-old," I marveled. "How did that make you feel?"

"It felt great!" Emmit was smiling as if he could still feel all those nickels and dimes weighing down his pockets. "It gave us a sense of pride. We learned, that day, how to make money, our own money. That, my friend, is a good feeling no matter what age you are. Motivation is the key. There has to be a reward for your effort. We wanted those cards and the spending money, so we were driven to succeed."

"When were you most motivated as a young man to succeed?" I asked. This, I believe, was the one question that personalized our time that day, though I am not sure where that question came from. It was certainly not in my list. I wonder if I was asking it for me and maybe for Billy. I wanted to know what level of motivation it took to make the sacrifices needed to succeed and take the risks that usually come with those sacrifices.

Emmit didn't hesitate with his answer. "Well, I certainly know the answer to that. I was 19-years-old and in my freshman year of college right here at Daytonville State. I met the woman of my dreams, Johnny. Someone so pretty, you know, your heart starts beating like it is going to explode out of your chest?"

He was giving emphasis and at the same time asking me if I had experienced this but delivered in a way that I knew my answer was not required, so he continued.

"Her name was Jenny Taylor, and she was the most stunning woman I'd ever seen. Over time, I worked up the nerve to talk with her. We spoke on the way to class, after class, and every free moment I could spend with her."

"She lived with her family off-campus and I lived on campus, I didn't have a car then and I knew if I wanted to take her out, I would need my own ride. So, after meeting her in my freshman year, I worked all summer, selling encyclopedias, door-to-door, trying to make enough money to buy a car. I can tell you," he confessed, "door-to-door-selling is a tough way to make money."

"Were you good at it?" I asked, even though I had a hunch Emmit was probably good at anything he had ever committed to doing.

"Not at first," he replied. "I didn't understand then that developing a skill requires the survival of trial and error; simple persistence. I was not good at selling when I began. My sample encyclopedias were merely heavy books to me. I hated carrying them around. They seemed boring to me so I did not see much value in them. I was about ready to give up and quit the job when I read one of the volumes."

I was intrigued and to be truthful, quite incredulous he would undertake the task. "What made you decide to read it before you quit?"

"It was a rainy day, and the encyclopedia company told salesmen not to carry their books out in the rain. Since selling books was not an option, I spent the day reading volume M, and to this day I can't tell you why I chose book M. I read about mandolins and mountain ranges. I read about Mexico, and then

I read about manatees. I flipped back-and-forth reading sections from the back of the book, then sections from the front, then from the middle. It was fascinating! I didn't read all of it at once. There wasn't enough time because the rain stopped after a stretch but I almost wished for more. I remember thinking everyone should have this information available to them."

"So you had to understand their true value before you could really sell them?" I offered drilling deeper into the initial question. I was just trying to do my job and ask the right questions, but as it turned out, if my polite handling of Misty showed Emmit I was a gracious person, this was the moment that confirmed to him that I was worth his mentoring. He could see I had not taken this interview for granted but came prepared with questions that, he would later tell me, no one had ever asked him. In looking back, I don't think I asked anything profound but he said I asked with such "excited curiosity," as he called it.

"That's exactly right, Johnny! Very good. I imagined an inquisitive child wanting to know about the world around them. I considered how educational the information was, and how it would help young people know what was in the world beyond their town and how it could inspire them to take part in it. In short, I knew people had to have this product. I knew it was good for them. With these books, I had valuable information and education to offer, and for people with children, I couldn't imagine them not having my product."

"So children were the key." I blurted. I began to understand how Emmit must have turned his sales around. If he knew who really needed the encyclopedias, he wouldn't be wasting time trying to sell people that did not have a need. He gave me a wink to let me know I was on the right track.

"The very next day I sold two full sets of encyclopedias, equal to what I had sold to that point all summer. I targeted my ideal customer—and indeed, you're correct—families with children. I looked for houses with bicycles and swing sets. I learned to sell and I sold well for the rest of the summer. I came to understand one key element for successful selling. I realized you have to want to brag about your product or service, otherwise you are not going to succeed in selling it. I confirmed an axiom that I have followed to this day: I do not want to be involved in a business if I cannot brag about what it offers customers."

"You have to want to brag about your offering," I paraphrased under my breath while jotting notes down on my pad of paper.

"This I know for certain: every entrepreneur is a salesperson, because you don't have a business if people don't buy your product or service. You have got to believe in what you are selling," Emmit continued with intensity in his voice, imparting a litany of qualities needed to succeed as an entrepreneur. "Have relentless energy, fueled by ambition, the daily self-discipline to perform the tasks most needed to be done and a desire to succeed in whatever you have chosen to accomplish." With a trailing warning, he concluded, "Starting a business is not for everyone."

"You have to have a good idea, right? Like the lemonade stand on hot days." I found myself wanting to participate, to learn. I wasn't sure if I was asking questions for me or for the article.

"I have come across business ideas over the years that were far better than mine, but failed miserably because the person with the idea simply lacked the perseverance and ambition needed to weather the storms that all new businesses face. I would bet on the success of a person with an average idea, who has aptitude and strong motivation to succeed, rather than someone with a great idea but lacking the qualities of a high achiever."

I opened up and started sharing with Emmit, "My father has worked hard every day of his life, but unfortunately we had very little to show for all that hard work, so I know one thing for certain: hard work is not the secret to success. He always did his best, but our family always struggled. There was always more month left than there was money in our house."

Emmit looked me in the eye and spoke slowly at first. "I admire your openness, Johnny. You remind me a little of myself when I was younger. I knew there would be a time when all I would have to offer was the willingness to work hard but at some point I would learn to exchange that hard work for working wisely."

It sounded like another rule he was sharing, but he just left it out there for me to discern its contents. He was ready to move on to the reward for his hard work. What earning the money for that car led to.

Chapter 5

THE LEGEND OF RED

J enny and I got married the summer before our third year, and I promise you the yes she gave me when I asked her to be my wife was the greatest sale I ever closed." He shared this with an expression of great accomplishment. "But with that 'yes' came the responsibility to take care of her, and that gave me the motivation I needed to work hard for a season."

I would learn later that Emmit believed working hard should only be for "a season" because working smart and leveraging every resource you have is what the wealthy do best.

"I worked in a grocery store stocking shelves in the evenings—pure hard work—and took classes during the day. I had the privilege at that grocery store one night to meet Red Davis. He cleaned the floor in our store and as I would later discover every other grocery store within 90 miles of

Daytonville. Let me correct myself. Red was the owner of a commercial floor cleaning company, and his employees did the actual cleaning. Red would be there some evenings to teach and encourage his employees. He was like watching Knute Rockne in action; except his football field was a hard vinyl floor."

I couldn't help but laugh at the image Emmit painted of this blue-collar man I had never met coaching his employees to pound those dirty floors into submission until they were clean.

Misty dropped off our chicken salad sandwiches and when she saw me laughing said, "He's a real charmer, ain't he?" But she could tell how engrossed we were in our conversation by that point, so she sped away again, offering me a little wink as she left.

"One night when Red was in our store and my work was finished early, I offered to help out. I loved to hear Red's tales; he was a great storyteller. Soon thereafter, I started working harder to finish my duties early every night so I could help his crew out. This impressed Red, and he began taking a liking to me, always teaching me something."

Did you talk about how to start a business?" I asked.

"No, it wasn't quite that formal. We talked about near everything. He would also ask me what my plans were for the future after graduation. I learned that he and his wife had two daughters that Red loved to spoil. I'm sure somewhere in his heart, he imagined his daughters taking over his business one day, but back in those days, business ownership was generally seen as a man's world. Red's success afforded his girls a good life, so I'm not so sure they had much interest in running a cleaning company anyhow. But it was during those evenings, intertwined in his stories, that I learned the power of entrepreneurship and its fruit… wealth. I was going to college learning how to make a living, and when he was there in the evenings, I was learning how to afford a great life."

I didn't understand the difference right away, and Emmit must have seen right through my look of confusion.

"Red was the one who taught me the difference between just making a living and wealth. He would say, 'Emmit, you see me here tonight cleaning,'—I always found that phrase funny because I actually never saw him cleaning—'but what you don't realize is I am also cleaning in Dakota, Rustburg and Millersville as well.' When he first said that, I could not quite figure that out, but it didn't take long to understand that having a well-trained employee he could trust allowed him to make money every time they were working."

He looked up for a moment to hail Misty, who scampered over and refilled his iced tea with a smile.

"You see, he taught me the power of passive income. I did not want to trade hours for dollars, specifically *my hours*, as my hours were limited with school and a new bride. My father and grandfather traded hours for dollars, and it never led to wealth."

"I asked—well, to be honest, I nearly begged—to come work for Red, which I did midway through my third year, working most evenings and full-time during the summer and winter breaks. That was my real education. He taught me the idea of saving a percentage of every dollar I ever made and a corresponding principle of giving a percentage of every dollar. I started those practices then and I continue to follow them today. I probably would have worked for him for free just to learn from him."

"But if you were working for Red, how did you become an entrepreneur?" That was the part I didn't get then, how you transitioned from working hard to working smart.

"Well," Emmit smiled, "part of starting to work smart is being ready to act on the right opportunity. Red became quite fond of Jenny and me. His daughters were happily married and their husbands were both set on climbing the ladder in big city jobs as he put it, so I think he had been thinking of me as his protégé for some time. At the close of my senior year, he presented me with an opportunity that I could not turn down, although I must say, most of my classmates thought I should have at the time. He suggested that I buy him out of his commercial floor cleaning business. Since he knew that Jenny and I did not have the funds to do this, he suggested a deal where I would give him a percentage of profits until our agreed upon figure was met.

"I turned down teaching jobs in larger cities, despite my new education degree, to pursue this opportunity, because it was my first step into entrepreneurship. It was a decision I have never regretted. Do you know why, Johnny?"

It was a question I knew he did not intend for me to answer, so I stayed quiet and let Emmit hold the moment with a look of excitement in his eyes.

"Because I have been a teacher to my employees since that very first summer when I took ownership of Advanced Floor Cleaning. It quickly grew profitable enough to pay for my wife to pursue an advanced degree without the pressure of having to work at the same time. Being financially independent gave me tremendous personal satisfaction."

Chapter 6

THE SEVEN PILLARS

I found myself nodding along with everything Emmit said, wanting to say less and listen more. I was so fascinated by his story. But I broke in and added, "It must have felt good to succeed as a young business owner."

"That's true, Johnny, it did. It also gave me the confidence to begin other businesses in the years following. In turn, I would offer opportunities to my employees much like Red offered me. I invited employees that had focused ambition, an area of expertise, and personal integrity to partner with me in new ventures or buy existing companies from me so I could focus on new endeavors."

This was the "Pied Piper" effect Billy had told me about. Somehow, I was wishing I was working for him, so I could earn one of those opportunities. I felt like I too had many qualities he valued in a partner, though I had yet to grow a single area of expertise. I knew, in time, I would and I set forth, from that day, to grow my knowledge level of the newspaper business.

"Emmit, I'd like to ask you … I don't know how much time you set aside today, but I am fascinated how someone can create their own income and the freedom that must provide." At that point, I was asking to use his knowledge for myself. In that moment, a spark was lit inside me, though I was not sure when my time would come to begin such a journey. I realized an opportunity sat before me that I could not miss because it might never present itself again. So in that moment, my questions and his answers, would be firewood set on the spark. I am certain the expression on my face and the tone in my voice hinted how valuable I believed the knowledge was that he could teach me. Through the wrinkles that appeared across his forehead, I could also see in his face a great deal of contemplation.

"Well," Emmit said after a moment of hesitation, pondering as though he was asking himself if I was worthy of what he was going to dispense. "The truth is, I believe there are seven axioms that need to be in place to build a successful business. I call them the Seven Pillars, and I consider each of them essential in order to build a company that can survive then thrive. Companies that are able to endure through changing economic times, competition, all sorts of other challenges that face new businesses. I know the stronger the pillars, the better a structure is supported—in this case the business."

At that moment, something in Emmit shifted. If it was possible, he became more enthusiastic. I wasn't just some reporter anymore I had become his student.

"When I said that I have been teaching ever since I bought Red's business, in fact, it is the Seven Pillars that I've shared with my key employees and new partners. And it has been their commitment to these principles that have created the success of our many ventures together."

"I cannot wait to hear them," I heard myself say, although to this day I am still not sure if I said it verbally or if it was just my body language that gave away the extent of my fascination with his subject.

"I'll start you with a brief overview. And if and when you do move forward into entrepreneurship, I would be happy to share them in greater detail with you at that time. I have already shared the **First Pillar**, though I didn't call it a pillar at the time," Emmit said. "***You must have the qualities of a high achiever***. Remember when I said a great idea in the hands of a person who lacks certain personal qualities would surely fail? The key point here is there are habits that high achievers have that cause them to succeed in most things they set out to do."

I wanted to be a high achiever. I hoped I could make their habits mine, although I was afraid what he was about to describe wouldn't sound like me at all.

"These qualities lead a person to establish a goal with a plan to accomplish it and, most importantly, have the self-discipline to take strategic action without delay every day to accomplish their goal. High achievers are motivated by these goals, because they have a clear vision of the payoff that provides the fuel to persevere. They have a positive mindset expecting to be successful. They are persistent viewing setbacks as only a temporary obstacle. They initiate action and have energy. In most cases, their energy seems never-ending."

This seemed to be a critical point for Emmit. His eyes weighted down a moment as he considered me carefully; as if he wanted to make sure I was still with him. As if this was where he had lost people before.

"Sadly, most folks only talk about what they want, then wonder why they didn't get it. High achievers also give off a sense of confidence that makes people *want* to follow them, and when you're starting a company, this is critical because you can't always pay high wages to new employees. These new team members come on board because they trust and believe in you; the leader. They believe you're going to achieve great things, and they will be a part of something big one day."

All the intensity Emmit had kept coiled up inside him unwound, for a moment at least. He took another sip of tea, like it was halftime or the seventh inning stretch.

"I am not saying a person needs all of these qualities, but I would not want to bet on the survival let alone the success of a business on someone who lacks too many of them. Johnny, give me someone with a clear dream, relentless energy and focused effort—and a big dose of unlimited optimism—and I will give you back a successful entrepreneur."

And with that, the greatest entrepreneur I had ever met finished enumerating the Seven Pillars. I still have the exact notes I scribbled on my legal pad that day framed and hung in my office, tea stain in the middle and all. These were the exact words I wrote down that day:

Emmit's 7 Pillars

1. You must have the qualities of a high achiever
2. Develop an active business plan
3. Protect yourself and your business
4. Recruit a team you can trust
5. Build a brand
6. Create systems
7. Know your numbers

Chapter 7

THE SECOND PILLAR

Over the next few years I was fortunate to share many more lunches with Emmit and even dinners with my wife Christine and his wife Jenny. Some time during our first year meetings, he shared that he and Jenny had no children though never giving a why. I thought maybe this was why he took a liking to me, teaching me principles of how to have a successful life. For some reason, I always believed—I have no sure answer as to why—he knew a dream was birthed within me during our first meeting and that he could foster it.

It would be nearly five years before that dream would go from a mere spark to a burning fire within me. This dream so excited me that it started waking me early in the morning and was the last thought in my mind before settling to sleep at night.

I asked Emmit if he would consider listening to a business idea I had. It was as if he had been expecting this moment, and with that our second most valuable lunch was scheduled

And at this meeting I would have in my hand the **Second Pillar**—*Develop an active business plan*, as I intended to plant the seeds of a partnership with Emmit. Specifically, I was going to ask him to provide or help raise the needed capital to buy our local paper, my employer—*The Daytonville Herald*.

He was our largest advertiser, and I had shared with him recently that the paper seemed to be struggling. But that day, I proclaimed with a degree of certainty (ascertained from being the senior editor after inheriting Billy Kincade's position following his long expected retirement), that one of two things was getting ready to happen: either the *Herald* would go under, resulting in him losing his leading source of advertising at the time, or a larger paper would buy it, increasing his ad rates and, of course, affecting his profit. Both of those outcomes, I was confident, would motivate him to consider my offer.

But what I believed was most attractive about this deal (and I knew from his stories that Emmit loved a good deal) was information I was privileged to learn from Billy before he retired. The Clancy family, who owned the *Herald*, wanted to sell to a local because they believed it was the right thing to do. I looked into the asking price and confirmed it was quite feasible since they would have a hard time showing a profit for quite some time. Most important was that, with a modest down payment, the balance could be paid over time. Those terms made for a doable deal, even for someone like me with nothing more than ambition, an opportunity and an insatiable appetite to learn.

SARA'S PART TWO

He was intrigued. So there we were at what I had now determined was his favorite lunch spot—Sara's Diner, at 12:45 just like our first meeting, the meeting that implanted in me the desire to be an entrepreneur.

When I walked up to him, he was glancing over the card, that simple white card that I had now seen a few times and that grabbed my curiosity at our first introduction. I was not sure if it was the same card from our initial meeting nearly five years prior, but it re-ignited my curiosity about its message once again. He quickly made eye contact, tucking the card away in his pocket and came to greet me with his usual warmth. However, I could tell instantly that this time there was a high level of focus.

While we were being directed to our seats he asked me, "The Second Pillar?"

"Of course!" I knew better than to come empty handed. "I have an active business plan that I think you will not only like, but may even want to be a part of." I planted nothing more than a seed I hoped would grow during the time to follow. It was one of Emmit's favorite techniques: planting ideas like seeds where you first till the land before the seed is planted and give it some time to grow. He first introduced me to this concept, explaining how too often ideas are shared like bullets, which often kill any chance the recipient will adopt.

We quickly placed our order as Emmit, with an intensity I had not experienced to this point, began asking me to defend the plan. So much for the subtle seed, I thought to myself. I felt like I was defending a dissertation. I was confident in this proposal. I knew what he expected in an active business plan as he had made it clear years before.

He had told me new business owners usually create a business plan to attract investors—more often than not friends and family—then they would never look at this document again after receiving the needed funds to start the business. "That type of plan is a static document. That's a huge mistake!" he declared.

Emmit agreed investors of any type deserve and expect to see a plan that confirms they will receive their investment back with a nice return. However, this plan needed to be "active" in that it would provide the road map the company would follow for the first two years, minimum. The plan was active because it was more than a static document.

This plan should declare why there was a need for the business in the market it would serve and how it would be different from its competition. Who could provide the expertise needed to oversee any area that required such experience? Would the costs versus the projected income provide a profit worthy of the risk and enough motivation to sustain its ownership through the tough times? He also wanted a declaration of what this company intended to be if all went well. He felt that many companies just survived and never set out from day one to actually dominate their market, to thrive and to become a giant.

I knew the most important question I needed to answer was what I was going to do differently than the previous owners that warranted his or anyone's investment dollars. My presentation confirmed that not only was this a good investment for him, as it would, in time, reduce his advertising costs for his existing holdings, but I shared a model that would increase our advertising base. We could maintain the *Herald*'s local feel while purchasing, at little cost, statewide, national, and even international stories that would rival the much larger *Chicago Tribune*.

Remember, those were the days before the Internet and even 24-hour cable news, when the paper was the most convenient and quickest source of news for most Americans.

I shared that I believed this model could be duplicated in countless smaller cities, featuring papers that would meet our standard metrics for potential acquisitions. The ability to duplicate, I deduced from my initial indoctrination into entrepreneurship, would be attractive to him and to others whom I hoped might participate as investors.

That would be just the first of many meetings over the next 6 to 8 weeks, but I admit it felt like only hours. My excitement merged weeks into what felt like a few days putting together a partnership that left all initially involved far wealthier in the years to come, all because I took action on my idea.

Chapter 8

THE THIRD PILLAR

W hen it all settled, Emmit and I would become the
largest shareholders. My stock would need to be
earned in the years to come—I called it sweat
equity, and I would go on to do all I promised, even exceeding
Emmit's lofty expectations. Because there were investors, some
silent and some with minor active roles, I learned how to apply
the **Third Pillar**—*Protect yourself and your business*.

In this initial planning period, Emmit would not allow a
launch without this due diligence being done. He shared with
me that too often partnerships are formed with great intention
by all parties only to end in great disappointment and a company
ruined because no one took the time to establish sometimes
simple, sometimes complicated partnership agreements that
would guide the company in the event a partnership ever needed

to be dismantled or reorganized. He asserted that a partnership agreement is one of a handful of girders that provide protection from a collapse. Like not having needed insurances or not establishing the proper legal framework of a corporation to protecting intellectual properties.

I can hear Emmit saying to me "the hope is you will never need all this protection, but in the event you do, you will be glad you took the time to protect yourself and the business."

PARTNERSHIPS

Emmit told me the story of a business he started with someone he believed was a good friend. Because of the friendship, he ignored his gut instinct to put an agreement together that, along with establishing ownership shares, would define each other's roles and accompanying responsibilities. With an agreement, responsibilities would have been determined by each other's strengths—his friend was more of a salesman and Emmit more of a systems and operations guy. This partnership agreement, along with its declaration of each partner's roles and correlating responsibilities, would have also featured the all-important buyout terms in the event either could no longer fulfill their responsibilities or stay with the company for whatever reason.

Emmit illustrated his point. "Our partnership worked well if—let's call him Jack—made the needed sales calls that resulted in new business and cultivated an on-going basic customer service relationship with our new accounts. My job was to make sure we had the staff in place to fulfill the requests of this new business. I would also handle our relationships with the bank and make sure our books were current."

Emmit let out a sigh and fidgeted with his napkin as he remembered the only time one of his partnerships failed. I could see in his face that recollecting this event was painful.

"This all sounds simple, but when we started growing and profit was plentiful, Jack stopped doing the things that made us successful. He found more hobbies than you can think of. At best, he'd bring a client along golfing to justify some of the time, then compound his poor judgment by making those countless outings a company expense. But that is another issue. Clearly this business relationship could not continue, but with no agreement in place, navigating the ending was relationally arduous and financially catastrophic for our company."

When I saw the painful look on Emmit's face as he recalled that failed partnership and—more importantly—lost friendship, I learned that the Third Pillar wasn't so much a day-to-day principle of running a business, but was an irrefutable pillar that had to be in place in the event you ever needed it.

Chapter 9

THE FOURTH PILLAR

I think I can remember every moment with Emmit during the first year of our partnership, especially our weekly meetings to review how we were implementing our active business plan. But what I remember as our key focus that first year was our work on the **Fourth Pillar—*Recruit a team you can trust*.**

If those first weeks of planning felt like days, our first year in business passed by in what seemed like just a few weeks, but I remember the recruitment of key team members to be paramount in our focus. Well, in fairness, Emmit's focus. He couldn't stress the "trust" part enough.

"Johnny," he shared, "you don't want to just hire people who can perform a task. Yes, there will be times when that will happen so you can open your doors to do business, but your goal should be bigger than just a hire to fill a need. Every hire can play a significant role in the success of the company because each hire brings an attitude and energy to work that, at the very least, will affect the culture of the company."

TOXIC INDICATORS

"And equally, every regrettable hire—and there will be some of those—will drain you and the team of its energy. Their contribution never equals their compensation. What you need to have in the interview process is alertness to *toxic indicators*."

It was an alarming combination of words and I only heard them used again one more time, years later.

I asked him to elaborate and he plainly told me some people are just negative. "No matter where you put them, they will complain to anyone willing to listen. When you or, in time, team members interview someone for employment— and, for that matter, anyone who may be joining your team in near any capacity, always ask the person why they are no longer with their last employer. If it is a potential partner, ask why they are no longer in the partnership. They will often, if prodded a touch, reveal this toxic indicator and it will be exposed as they blame someone or something for why there are no longer there.

At that, Emmit's eyes lit back up. He raised one finger in the air and gave it a triumphant shake.

"What you want is the person who says, 'It just was not the best fit. I wish my previous employer well. It was a good company, but I am looking for a new opportunity like this one with you.'"

MY STORY

Emmit encouraged me to develop a short story—my story; he called it—of why I wanted to start this company in the first place. It was, he felt, imperative early on for all new team members to know the vision I had for the company. The vision that I had shared with Emmit, which excited him enough to become a partner.

"You see, Johnny, your story will personalize the mission to each team member, and I've found people want to be a part of a mission, not just work at a job. Your story will also be important in establishing what I call the culture you will want."

Culture was paramount to Emmit. He believed that a work environment where everyone felt they made a contribution to the achievement of the overall mission allowed everyone, no matter what their position or role, to take great pride in the company.

Their pride was revealed in the quality of their work or contribution. In turn, their excellent performance created the trust. What he meant was that we wanted people who could carry out the mission without having someone look over them continually to assure the work was done right.

"It is too expensive to have never ending layers of management just to make sure people are doing their jobs," Emmit said. "So hire those you can trust with their time because labor is and has always been a company's greatest expense. This expense is never a waste if you have a team that gives a full day or more of focus to what they're doing."

THE CABINET

Along with our key employee hires that first year, what really stood out about building our team were the team members who were not employees, but the professionals that Emmit referred to often as our cabinet. He had trusted their council for years with his other companies.

The cabinet was made up of our accountant, banker, bookkeeper, lawyer and insurance guy, just to name a few. Their job, I learned, was to help protect our company against anything we might not see coming. Their advice was trusted and never ignored. It was not always followed because entrepreneurs, I would learn, at times must go with their gut over statistics, but that was a rare occasion.

This initial team positioned us to grow and, when the time was right, to grow fast.

Chapter 10

THE TEACHER

I n putting together our team, there was no more important team member than Amy Merrick.

Amy's story was a key part of what drove her to be so successful in her area of expertise. She married her high school sweetheart soon after graduation, only for him to leave her with two young sons for reasons I still have no clarity on, not that any excuse would justify him abandoning his young family. I always assumed her situation brought out her fierce survival mentality. Very early on, I knew she was tough as they come.

She started out as a part-time receptionist for one of Emmit's service companies, but she quickly moved up through various key positions to the point where he trusted her with anything that he knew had to get done. She had great capacity, a trait he valued equal only to trust. In her original part-time position answering the phones, she excelled taking note of why customers made the first call to his company and why they continued to call. She was organized and detailed; creating a daily log that charted all sorts of valuable information that she gathered just by asking customers for feedback. These questions helped her gather data that allowed her to suggest ways to make future advertising more strategic. It was no surprise Emmit brought her on full time as fast as he could.

She took on roles of increasing responsibility and had many titles, but as only Emmit could do in his plainspoken way, he explained her mission simply became to "get us some customers, make sure they keep using us and like us so much they tell everyone they know how good we are."

Emmit's broad-stroke description meant Amy was in charge of "advertising and customer experience" in her final role with him and his broad service business holdings, which allowed her to challenge anyone or anything in the service process that may have been a factor in a failed customer experience. Her job was to effectively advertise what the company could repeatedly deliver and she was not going to allow that promise to go unfulfilled. Customer experience was another new phrase that I learned and heard preached as gospel, which classified it as an "Emmit." That single word would come to describe anything Emmit declared was a definitive rule in life or business.

To say Amy was forced on the team would be an understatement, but no one in our first five years would be more valuable. I remember it like yesterday; Emmit with his slow, confident, request that you knew couldn't be refused.

"Johnny, I want you to meet someone who has been quite valuable to me and my businesses for more than a decade. Since I have a good bit in this new pot of ours, I am going to ask you to allow Amy to help us out as we get our footing. "

"Help us out" was either sarcasm or just his usual way of under playing what her contribution would be.

REVENUE

"My hope is Amy can assist us in the most important part of any new business," Emmit said, continuing his introduction. "That, my friend, is generating revenue."

And with that, she was in charge of all advertising and its fruits: revenue. I knew how to improve the content of our product and even had a few decent ideas on controlling costs and adding subscription revenue, but it was Amy who would be the savior of our floundering advertising revenue stream.

Emmit wanted to ring the bell one more time for emphasis, declaring definitively, "The number one reason new businesses fail, they run out of cash. And the reason they run out of cash," he paused, letting the answer hang in the air, "is because they do not bring in enough revenue to pay the expenses needed to operate the business, let alone enough to satisfy the owners' income desire for taking the risk of starting the business in the first place. When either of those things happens, businesses close their doors.

"I've heard the fancy term they were under-capitalized, but if they brought in the needed revenue from the start, they would not have needed the additional capital to survive."

With Emmit, every lesson was a rung on a ladder.

Chapter 11

THE FIFTH PILLAR

After we took ownership, *The Herald* under Amy's leadership began to partner with our advertisers, advising them on what, in her experience, proved to be effective. When I say effective, I mean we had a standard. In fact, we had a much higher standard, as we believed effective advertising branded a given company in the mind of a consumer.

That is a tall order, but in my first meeting with Emmit—that simple lunch that planted the seed of my awakening—he shared with me briefly his key thought about the **Fifth Pillar—** *Build a brand.*

"A brand is the one thing a customer can count on when experiencing your product or service. The challenge, of course, is to first identify the one thing that is most important to your customers that your competition is not delivering." Delivering a strong warning, he added, "and your company better be able to deliver on what you're promising, repeatedly."

It was in Emmit's first introduction of this pillar to me that he emphatically declared, "The great entrepreneurs make audacious promises, like Henry Ford wanting to manufacture a car that near everyone could afford. One sentence, big promise! But this big promise guided his company for decades. It is why Ford developed the assembly line and used it more effectively than any other automaker. It is why black was the only color car you could purchase from Ford for so long."

Emmit believed a brand could be built, by a company, by dedicating itself to that one big foundational promise. "Building a brand from day one is so critical for new business owners," he said. "It gives them a target in who they will strive to be as a company. Henry Ford and the assembly line and his fascination with black allowed him to manufacture automobiles at less cost and in turn sell cheaper. But both of those strategies were outgrowths of the brand he first set out to create: an affordable automobile. They helped him make good on his promise."

Emmit closed his original thought with a charge. "Ford's claim, I am sure, as it did with my father, sat in the minds of every American worker. If I work and make a livable wage, I can own a car that will give me convenience as well as the freedom to go anywhere. His promise made every part of our great country reachable."

THE FIFTH PILLAR IN ACTION

It was through Amy that I first saw the Fifth Pillar and its influence up close. From the beginning, with no college training in marketing or business, just her jousts with Emmit, she crafted branding messages with singular promises that could be delivered by his companies and be the centerpiece of advertising campaigns. It was obvious she learned the effectiveness of *building a brand* as the long-term approach to advertising. For this reason, she established branding as the catalyst we would use for our advertisers in any advertising plan.

Amy was emphatic we did not just sell advertising space. Our approach would be more exhaustive as we developed a system for our advertising consultants, the title she gave to those who in fact were responsible for selling ad space. In the beginning, their titles even confused me as their job was to sell, after all, but she stressed we were going to do more and do it differently.

ONE-SIDED SELLING

Emmit knew the value of a new business—or for that matter any-age business—being able to sell its offerings so he fully supported Amy's approach to helping our customers' brand through advertising. He encouraged me to let Amy execute her strategy, articulating his own experience.

"We have heard the carnival barkers enticing you to participate or the car salesman, listing all the features of a car in a fashion similar to an auctioneer. Both illuminate the one-sided selling approach—one side gives as many benefits as needed to overcome the opposition who then submits and purchases."

Emmit pulled out his worn billfold. It looked like he had owned the same one for decades. From it, he pulled an old black and white picture of Jenny, from just after he married her.

"One-sided selling is like meeting a young lady you fancy and on your first date together, you ask her to be quiet while you list for her all the reasons she should like you." He started to laugh. "How well do you think that will work for you? Do you think I ever could have used that foolish approach to garner a yes from this beautiful young lady?"

His point was obvious. People want to discover why they like something and not be told why they should like it.

He knew Amy realized that telling a potential advertiser with *The Herald* what they need would often bring along a reluctant buyer who was "convinced" by overwhelming information that a purchase is good or that they need it. That type of selling does not lend itself to attracting an advertiser who is patient enough early on to allow for the needed adjustments in regards to proper ad placement and frequency.

What happens in these one-sided sales effort—I call it the "convincing approach," you bring on a reluctant buyer often because you over-promise results. That is a critical error made by most sales people. They simply keep adding promises until the hearer gives up. What you end up with is expectations that rarely, if ever, can be met. What you have done is attracted short-term advertisers. I would not even call them clients because there was no initial relationship built or understanding of the company or the individual who was being sold.

And with that, our sales process and its execution, using Amy's style of asking questions (she called it her "discovery process"), became instrumental in our consulting approach to selling advertising. Our first emphasis was on identifying what our client's brand was or would be and crafting messages with supporting promotions, sales and the like instead of just taking sales orders.

THE HUB

Amy, always the trainer with the most pleasant of smiles, professed, but more importantly illustrated, that the brand needed to be the "hub" and the taglines, events, sales and promotions would be the means, the "spokes," to promote or build the brand. So the brand was the hub and the branding efforts were the spokes. The "hub and spokes" was one of endless metaphors she used to illustrate how she believed branding worked in relation to an advertising campaign.

In this model, the methods of advertising just facilitated the actual branding. Her approach reversed the old world order when the sale, promotion or event was why a business used the paper as the advertising means.

She held to the conviction that we were stewards of our client's hard-earned profit, so let's not sell them anything. Let's assist them in establishing a branding message that differentiates them from their competition. "Who are they as a company and what repeated promise, experience or quality can the consumer count on from them?" I must have heard her ask that 100 times during the early sales trainings I initially sat in on.

I found it fascinating how she forced her advertising consultant to ask questions and listen. How she stressed, let me get the wording correct, "aggressive listening." Finally, and only after this asking and listening could our advertising consultants and clients begin to work together, in a joint effort, to discover the most deliverable *promise, characteristic, value or attribute* the company could confidently and repeatedly provide to customers.

After our discovery process, we worked with our advertisers to think through and narrow the chosen brand to what their customers would most want in a company that sold their product or service and that their competition was not already providing.

All these touch points needed to be reached and we found this progression could not be done by a "good talker," a quality that had been sought out in the past for the old *The Daytonville Herald* sales representatives. No, this process could only be done by someone who could aggressively listen, then co-create with the company a branding message followed ultimately by making decisions about strategic placement and frequency.

ONE SIZE DOES NOT FIT ALL

For every client, Amy stressed how the promise could be different. "The durability of a toolmaker is paramount for tradesmen, but the speed of delivery on an ordered product through a mail order catalog may be the promise we need to promote for our advertisers selling a product through the mail."

Along the same lines, she said a barber may promise that a customer will never wait more than 15 minutes to get a reasonably priced haircut. Each company needed to know what promise they could repeatedly deliver. I grasped that repeated delivery was a non-negotiable. It had to be something the advertising company understood was not just a wish, but a firm reality.

Moving on to our final component in the process, ad placement and frequency, Amy believed "placement should be determined by the 'who.'" I took note of her delivery of the word "who" because Amy and Emmit, both when attempting to show emphasis or persuade your thinking, would pause before and after a key statement. I noticed the key word or statement was always delivered in a softer tone, forcing the listener to be attentive. Amy might have been a "brand person" and Emmit might have been an "operations and strategy guy," but they both had great communication skills—another quality I learned a leader of any organization would be wise to develop into an asset.

THE WHO

Demographics was a term Amy rarely used, preferring "who." "Who is most likely to buy the product or service?" she asked as if we were her class, though it was only the four of us.

She repeated it like a drill sergeant. "Who is most likely to buy their product or service?" Then she'd answer her own question with a deepening question. "Will it be a male or female, young or old and do they need to be rich to be able to afford it?"

The answer to these questions would determine the segment of the population—in fact, the demographics.

Understanding a company's target audience would allow us to place their ads in locations that would attract the readers who were most likely to use the service or product being advertised.

"A barber would do well in the sports section, which has a male dominated reader, where a dress maker should be placed in our 'Best Recipes of the Week' section, which shares the secrets to fixing a casserole, a Sunday dinner, and a dessert recipe." Amy left nothing to chance, creating a process that delivered the highest probability of success for our advertisers.

All of this might not sound revolutionary today, but it was unique at the time to actually ask questions before you wrote up an order. It worked well for us. As a matter of fact, we were so steadfast in our process that if we did not think the concluding chosen brand and its message or supporting advertising elements would be effective, we would politely pass on your business and encourage you to try something else that would be a better fit.

Yes, we turned away business because what we did not want was the business owner, sitting in a barber's chair or at the diner with folks to the left and right of them, sharing for all to hear how they were persuaded to place an ad in our paper and it did nothing.

Over time, I developed a better understanding of the Fifth Pillar and all the tentacles that extended from it. I learned that advertising is providing the needed information to attract as well as retain customers and the methods ranged from TV, newspaper and radio advertisements to sponsoring a local sports team with your company's name on the back of the shirts.

Too often, because a long-term brand was never chosen or a message was never conceived, businesses' advertising becomes a hit or miss method of trying various vehicles, hoping to find the one that attracts enough customers to, at the very least, cover the cost of the advertising. I learned *break-even* is too low of a bar for any company to set.

Companies too often put their focus on the advertising vehicle instead of the message that differentiates the company from their competition. And with such a shortsighted approach, a key component in an effective advertising program demographics, the "who" is not even brought into the equation.

Amy would share with me that most companies advertising plans were similar to flying a kite. If the wind blew enough that day, it was a good day. So if something worked that month, the business owner would declare it a hit, close their eyes and continue doing it. That is, until they decided to track it again when they may find out that it is no longer working, and so the process would begin anew of searching for another "hit" that attracts customers.

The only method more amusing than this is the "word of mouth" method haled too often by older companies whose owners claim they are so good that people just sit around and brag about their company so much that people hear it and seek this legendary company out. Ok, I am exaggerating a bit, but as Emmit once said, "Everyone needs people to share their good experiences about their company, but I have rarely found it will create enough new buyers for the company to grow."

And by grow, Emmit meant exponential growth in either your existing location or duplicating what you presently have in new cities. For that level of growth to happen, he reiterated one of the lessons he taught me at our very first lunch—the need for customers from three areas: new customers, repeat customers and word-of-mouth referrals."

Chapter 12

GAME CHANGERS

I look back at all of our game changing hires in our early years when survival was our goal and David Gibbons was certainly one of those. We were nearing our third year or so in business and David was an intern that summer, assisting with print ad production. He desperately wanted to continue in the fall with us, but his schedule included a full academic load at Daytonville State, which did not lend itself to the daily rituals of print media.

Amy and I both liked him—for that matter, I think everybody liked David—so I remember giving him a task that was near impossible for someone two years removed from high school. He, however, had the confidence to make me think he could just as well succeed.

The project specifically was a two-page spread, which is simply two pages facing each other with a larger banner headline. My hope was that the ads we could sell surrounding the content would be an income generator. He had 25 days to work with our reporters on what content the spread should include and, most importantly, he would generate revenue through advertising sales.

He came up with a niche piece that would feature articles that reflected the personalities, culture and how-to advice. The idea was that the content would be drawn out of interviews with local folks. The initial topics ranged from how to grow a garden to the three musts for a perfect summer picnic. The upside was that this new content had the potential to make money, which was often like a dirty word in the print media world.

Yes, Emmit often reminded me, making money is why you're in business in the first place. I would ask myself this simple question often as I learned that too often in business we do things that are not profitable. I became a numbers savant over time, knowing the costs and profit margins on near anything related to our business.

With that said, the cost to try this new content was minimal, but David did not need to know that. He was accustomed to seeing each page in the paper flanked with strategically placed ads that had been purchased so it made no sense to lower the standard.

Yes, another Emmit: "You don't need to tell your employees everything as some information is best kept to only those who need to know. Rarely is that everyone."

The first time he graced me with that Emmit, I looked shocked, as if he was asking me to lie. He clarified in a light-hearted tone. "Sometimes, information needs to be given in doses. Sometimes you just need to get them up on the bike by giving them enough information to get started. Not giving them all the information is your way of holding the bike steady as they learn to peddle while balancing. Once you can tell they can handle the assignment or be trusted with information, then you give them more."

David was smart enough to ask Amy for help creating a script of what he would use in his initial call to potential advertisers. He was handcuffed because his list of targets was narrow and most had been called on endlessly over the years with no success. Amy, who oversaw the potential list that he would call on, chose businesses she thought would be a good fit, but at that point we had not compelled to advertise yet.

AMBITIOUS, COMPETITIVE, FOCUSED AND A LEARNER

David confirmed the validity of the First Pillar, exemplifying the qualities of a high achiever, though he was not a business owner (at least not yet). He had ambition with a desire to learn. He did not only want to master the skill of selling as he was competitive and that was obvious, but what I noticed and I liked was that he took the initiative to expand his view of the initial assignment, becoming a learner.

He understood the need for a quality product. The better the product, the easier the selling would be so he enlarged his focus to include product development, from ad placement to ad pricing. He thrived in our environment of freedom where his strategic use of focused energy (my phrase to express that ambition alone is not enough) allowed him to succeed.

With Amy's approval, he quickly changed the name of clients that bought space in this new feature to *sponsor advertisers*. Some businesses, he learned—and most were old-time businesses—relied on word of mouth as their only means to obtain customers, so they liked this new wording. It made them feel like they were supporting the community, not buying customers.

Before long, I found myself looking forward to reading this monthly "pocket full of sunshine" as it just made you glad you lived in a town like ours when you read it. You realized great people with great knowledge, which they shared in a folksy way, just wanted to pass on what they had learned over the years.

Competitive Advantage

"Just Daytonville" became the name of David's niche piece and it would grow beyond a two-page spread. The name and format, we knew with just the simple interchange of the town or city name, could be duplicated. Opportunities to duplicate were something I had begun to look for. We knew "Just Daytonville" and its simple model was profitable and, in time, became a lynchpin in all our papers, bringing together our original mission of *a local paper you wanted to read because it kept you informed of all things local, but brought with it the select national and world news that everyone needed to be informed of.*

We acquired two additional small town papers in year four, which allowed us to test if our model paper with its boutique approach of balancing local, national and world news was a winner. We believed this balance gave us a unique product at the time with a perfect synergy. We believed it actually gave us a competitive advantage over larger market papers that, except for the name of the local sports teams, all looked the same with the dominant content being world and national news.

We were trying to create the perfect newspapers, more valuable to their readership than giants like *The New York Times* or *Chicago Tribune*, which I came to believe we could do if it was our goal. Maybe it was the former athlete in me, but I don't remember ever competing in a sporting event where my goal was just to participate. No, my goal was to do my very best so my team could win so why should business be different, I thought.

Chapter 13

LEADERSHIP 101

With growth came new divisions and titles within our company. One new division we put under Amy was subscription sales. But what we learned is that we needed someone different. If I give credit where credit is due, it was Amy who, within 90 days of being given this new responsibility said, "All sales are not the same and you need a cheerleader for this position."

She explained what she meant by a cheerleader. "This is far from a consultant sale and needs someone who can be creative with promotions and motivation." And with that, she was quick to remove herself and promote someone from her staff to run this new division.

In Amy Merrick, I saw first-hand leadership exemplified in her handling of that new responsibility. She knew what she was good at and what her staff could do equal to or better than she. It was Amy who shared with me how she kept a cheat sheet, as she called it, in her desk drawer of every key responsibility and position within her oversight.

Her cheat sheet was similar to a baseball lineup card, something I was all too familiar with. Hers, however, contained who she thought could handle any area or position at some point, if needed.

"When the crisis happens," she said, explaining her logic to me, "and someone leaves or you need someone to step up and take something from you, you don't want to be making that decision the day the fire starts."

THE THREE P'S

Amy's advice on knowing your own—as well as your team's—strengths and capacity seamlessly led to her next lesson on leadership. Thinking back now, she truly was a teacher at heart. I began to parallel her voice with Emmit's, knowing her insights were distilled from her years under his watchful guidance.

"Too often companies have ALOT problem." I remember asking her to repeat this, thinking she was telling me we have a lot of problems, but she said "not a lot, ALOT!" It was an acronym.

"ALOT—*a lack of talent* under your leadership when you don't hire the right people, either because you can't identify or attract them. And if you're lucky enough to stumble on talent, you don't promote those people fast enough to something challenging so you lose them."

She shared with me often that leaders, and more often managers, may need to release a responsibility sooner than they want, to someone who has the three P's. Yes, with Amy there was always a catchy phrase, story, list or acronym so you never forgot what she was telling you.

Ah, the three P's, one of Amy's most memorable lessons. If someone under you had a *passion* to do something, the ability and eye for detail to do it *perfectly* and the *perseverance* needed to excel, a leader would be wise to move that standout to the front of class and get them leading.

"Perfect?" I asked. Do they really do it perfectly? I thought to myself incredulously, that seemed to be a bit unrealistic of a standard, but her response laid my doubt to rest.

"Ok, tell me how well you want them to do something," she requested. I thought for a minute and my long pause gave away the answer.

"You see," she said, "employees with the three P's automatically try to execute assignments perfectly because winners naturally set a standard higher than the others. And, if you think about it, what other standard is acceptable? Do you want someone whose work you always need to check to find out what they missed? Perfect just means you don't need to worry, when delegating a task to them, because these special individuals check over their work themselves."

When Amy got on a roll with one of her lessons, you just had to let her run, and it was always worth your time. "You can't wait with someone like that. They get bored too quick. They need a challenge to keep them engaged and, if you're lucky, they can do your job."

This, I knew, she learned from Emmit because her next statement gave away the payoff.

"If you're an entrepreneur, there are few things more valuable than someone who can now do a job you are currently doing. That lets you focus on what great entrepreneurs do best—think up another profitable idea and start the process all over."

This was one of countless lessons I learned, not just from Emmit, but also from all of his team members because he was kind enough and, in truth, wise enough in our early years to apply the Fourth Pillar to our partnership—*recruit a team you can trust.* He lent our partnership his key staff to lead something short-term and longer where required, which provided much needed support.

I was never quite sure how long he planned for Amy to stay, but to my good fortune he never brought her back. This allowed her to lead our Advertising Sales Department as a disciple of Emmit's Fifth Pillar, *build a brand,* for over a decade. He knew better than anyone that she had the three P's our new venture needed. And those, of course, were passion, perfection and persistence.

Chapter 14

THE SIXTH PILLAR

The **Sixth Pillar** — *Develop systems*, would become a priority in how we operated our business. I believe it was this one discipline that allowed us early on to have such success with the failing small newspapers we acquired.

I was on the alert from day one to look for patterns and processes that produced successful results. During the time leading up to our launch and the mentoring to follow, Emmit stressed the value of developing systems. It was, in fact, one of his greatest strengths. Systems in business, I learned, are processes that, when followed to specificity, resulted in a favorable and, most importantly, repeatable outcome. This axiom allowed, possibly greater then any, exponential growth to be achieved as it maximized the organization's talent force.

This was one of the more technical pillars, but he taught it to me in what seemed like a parable. I remember him pointing to a picture of one of his favorite desserts on the menu at Sara's Diner.

"Let us take this award-winning apple crumb cake, as it's referred to under its picture. Someone, somewhere made it first, and I would venture its recipe has been loaned to others who have attempted to make it. I would be willing to further bet that on many occasions, it did not turn out award winning," he said with a laugh, "even though all the attempters had the same written recipe." This is when Emmit paused, which meant it was the moment he was about to plant the seed. "Now why is that?" he asked.

Knowing his style by that point, I knew the question was not meant to be answered, only to lay the foundation for the lesson to follow.

"I am no Betty Crocker," he began (I still find it amusing that people believe this is an actual person, when in truth it is just a master piece of branding by its owner General Mills), "but I am willing to bet I can get this award-winning apple crumb cake from a brand new kitchen worker who has a desire to succeed."

Here, he interjected an Emmit. "I say they need desire because there is nothing you can do with a person who has a condition I call I don't give a…" He paused, lowering his tone, "S-H-I-T." To be honest I am still not sure I heard the actual T come out, but I got the message clearly. The way he had to spell the word still makes me laugh, as foul language was not a regular in his vocabulary. This simple truth, because of that one memorable word from him, resulted in my ownership of this principle after hearing it only this one time.

"So," he continued, "assuming I have the person with a touch of desire to do something correctly, with the use of a system our new kitchen worker would bake this award winning apple crumb cake. The system would be fairly simple, as it would first require that I had the complete written recipe with all the specifics such as ingredients, amounts and steps required. But, like I said, that alone is not enough. What is needed is *training*.

"Training would allow our new kitchen worker to see, first hand, someone who knew how to prepare this recipe, bake it successfully. This visual learning would be followed by my new kitchen worker attempting to bake the award-winning apple crumb cake themselves, with an instructor present, who would answer any questions that might arise during this attempt. That is comprehensive training, which will result in a repeated successful outcome."

"Too often business owners give up on a system, claiming it didn't work. If it didn't work, it was because the recipe was not complete from the start or they did not provide adequate training or, as I said from the beginning, you had a participant who simply did not care about succeeding."

Now Emmit was ready to take his system beyond apple crumb cake and on to the entire menu, which was a key point about developing systems. They were strongest when they could be replicated.

"If every recipe on that menu was a system with all the elements I suggested, this restaurant could duplicate itself in any targeted city or just sell the system for baking that award-winning apple crumb cake. That, my friend, is how you become wealthy as an entrepreneur."

Chapter 15

THE MANAGER

I learned early on that entrepreneurs should consider recruiting someone on their team who is a stark contrast to them. Where one person thrives in the creation of a business, another person will have great value as the operator of the created organization. Their gift is not in igniting, but in administration or managing an organization and all the details that encompass it. With that, I introduce Martin McCallister, our Vice President of Operations and Finance. Yes, in our early years it was common to oversee more than one area, as capacity was a much-heralded quality in our organization. Martin was a loveable curmudgeon. I love that word, and in my brief writing career I have had rare occasion to use it, but Martin personified it.

He was "The Manager"—his uniform (as even his clothes reflected his need for repetition and systematic order) of choice was always grey slacks of one shade or another, a short sleeve white dress shirt with his black eye glass case fixed in the left chest pocket, and the ever present dark tie. Affixed to his boxed face were black impenetrable plastic-rimmed glasses. Most noticeable was what was hinged to his thick black belt—an industrial keychain containing, I can only guess, keys to gain access to every door or lock he had ever needed to open in his lifetime. Those keys clanged when he walked, allowing you to hear his approach from well in the distance.

He was one of my early hires. We had completed only two small acquisitions prior to his arrival. By that point, though, I had begun confirming to myself my personal strengths, weaknesses and capacity so I knew I needed someone who obsessed over the details. And Martin did.

Martin served a term in the military straight out of high school. When that stint was over, he then spent nearly 25 years rising from entry level to plant manager of a textile plant in a neighboring county. He was looking for new employment because, he said, asking that the information he was about to share remain confidential, he did not think his current employer would survive much longer. He drew this conclusion, I am sure, with mathematical certainty because orders had become smaller and less frequent over the last few years.

I shared my story; the one Emmit encouraged me to create, as well as the make-up of our investment group and its ability to provide the company any needed capital, if required. I sensed it necessary to overcome his initial skepticism and innate caution in hopes of gaining his enlistment to our team. This hire required multiple meetings over a couple weeks, but from the very first meeting I made it no secret that his strengths were my weaknesses and that I was certain he would bring much needed value to our young company.

I could tell my openness validated to him that he was wanted and would provide a much needed skill set. This tool, of openly expressing someone's potential value to our company, I kept in my toolbox and would use often over my tenure to recruit anyone who I believed was a missing piece of our constantly changing talent puzzle.

Like all great hires, I would learn you feel their presence from day one and see their value quickly. Martin was one of my team members early on that I was so glad I did not pay by the hour. Like me, he was a first in and last out player. It was obvious to everyone he was a pack mule with the gift of organization. His office quickly mirrored that of a military command center with charts, graphs, rosters and maps with our current three newspaper locations as well as acquisitions he learned we were considering identified by color-coded thumbtacks, not to mention a wall of coded calendars, and finally—rounding out his arsenal—every new calculating device he could put his hands on.

Our business, like all daily papers, was a hostage to deadlines. But after hiring "The Manager," I knew those deadlines and every correlating task would never pass unfulfilled.

MANAGER VERSUS ENTREPRENEUR

Martin indeed was a manager and stood in stark contrast to Emmit and, I hoped in time, me as well. Being different was not a bad thing, it was just reality. Emmit embodied forward thinking, dreaming and calculated risk taking with the ability to teach and motivate others to join his mission and make it their own. By the time Martin came on board, I believe Emmit's influence on me was apparent. I was learning how to teach and motivate and I was beginning to have my own vision of the future of the company.

Martin, however, was none of the above. He believed people fulfilled responsibilities because they were paid and instructed to do so, and if they did not they needed to be removed from the equation. He preached there was a reason why "risk was a four-letter word." Finally, he would not move comfortably forward with anything that contained any unknown variable. He wanted to leave nothing for chance.

I have not met anyone prior to his hiring or since who relished making sure something would work with exact precision, which made overseeing our systems a natural for him. In fact, to even become an approved system, Martin had to have concluded, with data, that the "four musts" of any system were met. There was (1) a formula (2) that could be taught and, if so, that produced outcomes that were (3) predictable and (4) profitable. "Profitable" could not be ambiguous, but measurable by saving time or money with its implementation.

Martin, as if being asked to translate a historical document, took prodigious effort in providing the most valuable piece of any continuing system—the training material. I stressed to him that our training needed to be simple and streamlined. Simple was not a word in his vocabulary, but he met the challenge delivering for all our approved systems a guidebook for teaching that contained all the processes, procedures and rules for operating. Thanks to Martin's guidebooks, we could duplicate the training formula successfully for decades to come.

Entrepreneurs are rarely detailed and, more often than not, normally have a sketch of what they want and believe could happen. This sketch, often reflecting an idea, could serve as the catalyst for the unbelievable to take place. I, for one, am a convert to the belief that managers help the implementation of these ideas so they can become functioning businesses. And, for sure, they are necessary to operate the systems that allow a good initial business to grow and become great businesses.

THE BRIEFER

I had always pictured someone with very little personality, maybe it was the chief of staff or I had heard once someone called "the briefer," who gave threat assessments to the President of the United States first thing each morning. The goal, I speculated, was to alert the president to the dangers of the world he was actually waking up to. This, I can only imagine tempered his ambitions and optimism with reality.

Martin was my morning messenger sharing with me anything that could become a problem. He also analyzed, with hard numbers and his usual skepticism, all the new ideas and potential acquisitions we considered. His job was to tell me if the numbers supported the probability something could be done and, if so, what were costs and how long would it take to make it *breathe*—my term for the day it is operating.

I do think he worked from an initial position of skepticism always searching for the level of risk and loss potential. But what I liked was how he delivered hard data to me, not opinions. His weapons of choice were charts, graphs and reports. These, he always presented as the 10 or never less than five reasons why the idea, acquisition and sometimes dream would not work.

His information would result in me and our board, which was our investor group, making decisions based on the numbers and facts, not emotions and wishful thinking. These, I learned quickly, are never a good criterion for a major decision and, in truth, any decision. The good news was, when a proposal could not be brought crumbling to the ground in these morning jousts, I could present to our investors a proposal that would withstand the usual barrage of questioning. Instead of investor doubt, our proposals garnered excitement, which allowed us to begin moving swiftly into our growth phase acquiring targeted newspapers.

EXPANDING

I had a firm foundation of senior level management with Martin and Amy and tested systems that we had great confidence in. Our team understood and bought into our mission. Finally, our ownership was in full support of our vision and confident we had all the needed safeguards in place. It was our time to grow.

After year five, we began to stretch, growing our stable by adding a newspaper that met our criteria for acquisition every quarter.

It was Emmit, becoming more involved again during this time, who expanded our investment group, which provided much-needed capital for growth. The sage thrived in his role as a rainmaker, as only he could speak with the authority and conviction of a seasoned entrepreneur. He garnered tremendous respect and connected well with our potential participants. We found with his help, new investors were plentiful, which afforded us the opportunity to aggressively begin purchasing family or locally owned small papers.

We determined our strike zone was towns with a minimum of 20,000 and no more than 60,000 deliverable households (defined as potential subscribers who could receive our daily paper), but where daily subscriptions were only delivered to a small fraction of potential subscribers. This gave our subscriptions sales division an initial goal of increasing subscriptions by 10% within 90 days of our acquisition with staggered increases over the first 18 months. That was an ambitious goal, but goals needed to be specific. They had to be challenging but obtainable with a clear plan set by the leadership group, which means from ownership to managers. I was a firm believer that ambitious standards either motivated team members or eliminated ones who didn't buy in to the newly set destination.

Chapter 16

THE SEVENTH PILLAR

The **Seventh Pillar** — *Know your numbers*, I first learned the value of years earlier presenting the Second Pillar, my active business plan, to Emmit to gain his initial involvement and investment. It was during this inquisition that I became knowledgeable about which numbers were real and which ones were completely wishful thinking, as Emmit believed most numbers featured in a business plan projection were fantasy. What he meant was that projections can't be what you think or want them to be, they must be underpinned by actual numbers that could be defended as if in a legal trial.

Assuring our company experienced growth and operated profitably was my primary responsibility. It could be shouldered by my team, but could not be delegated.

Emmit distilled to me from the outset, "Johnny, I am here to help where I can for as long as I can. If you assemble the right team they will surely help make the journey easier, but someone has to give the destination and hold everyone accountable for reaching it and that person, my friend, is you.

"If you're lucky, you'll surround yourself with a board of folks who have flown higher than you and faster than you so they can assist you in those critical decisions. There will be less of those critical decisions than you think, but when they arise it is not a decision you want to make alone."

But what I could not blame anyone for was not knowing or managing the cash flow. He told me I needed to know what our costs were, and he meant every single cost, so we knew how much to budget to run the operation every day, every week and every month. This was my paramount responsibility, and Emmit implored me that no one would have a greater interest in the cash flow, expenses or for certain profit than me.

"You need to know how high you have to jump to get over the hurdles," he said. "Too often, business owners let those hurdles turn into high jumps, which is pure stupidity or laziness because high jumps require a whole lot more effort and skill to get over."

Emmit, it was clear, liked his hurdles to look more like simple little rain puddles he could step over without even a jump, so long as he could see them. He also liked cash, lots of cash, but not the kind he spent on himself. He was a fan of cash reserves, money you could put your hands on the day you need it.

He indoctrinated me with his view of cash, imparting to me, "Johnny, your company's income must exceed its expenses and, I would argue, exceed expenses to the point that you can systematically create a sizeable cash reserve that can bring you through a slow period as well as fund times of expansion. If ever you find the company is not meeting expenses or is unable to create this reserve fund, you have a *toxic indicator* and every alarm in your head should be sounding that this must be fixed immediately. This was only the second time I had heard him use the term toxic indicator, so this principle became a commandment I would never forget, reinforced by equating cash to oxygen—without it you die!

DASHBOARD SYSTEM

In time, our numbers would sprout and the amount of things I needed to be aware of seemed endless so I relied heavily on our finance office and its staff. At its helm now was Jane Becket, taller than average with a lanky build and a trademark grey ponytail that provided her a clear view of all that was in front of her. Like her mentor Martin, she also might have lacked a little in the personality department, but thrived in obtaining and presenting numbers. Jane's office was responsible for running my dashboard system—something I created after Emmit's exhortation regarding toxic indicators—as well as every critical number we needed to be alert to. The dashboard operated much like the one in my automobile, which put directly in front of me every major measurable I needed to know that my trusty Oldsmobile was operating correctly and—if something was not operating correctly—turned on lights directly in front of my view to alert me of any problem soon to come.

Some numbers I needed to see weekly. In fact, early on when cash flow was the tightest, Martin gave me some near daily. By the time we hit our growth phase, most were given to me each week on Wednesday. Some numbers I only needed to see monthly and some I only wanted occasionally, for strategic reasons, when considering an expansion or acquisition.

I have to admit, I was obsessed with numbers and Jane fed my addiction. I had learned that successful entrepreneurs don't actually take foolish risks, as some have come to believe. In fact, they look at all the information available and then they take calculated risks that they believe are manageable.

Chapter 17

EXIT STRATEGIES

I had the great luxury of Amy leading her advertising sales group and creating its ground breaking sales training system for a decade and two years. Her excellence afforded me time that I did not need to spend concerned with our advertising revenue and this I knew was a great privilege to anyone building a business. When she moved on, I would be lying if I said I did not miss her presence for so many reasons, but I also knew it was the right time for her.

Her time working for Emmit and the excitement we experienced re-launching a town fixture like *The Herald*, ignited a fire within her that she could only fan through entrepreneurship.

She took the big leap remarrying and moving to Chicago when her youngest child, Gordon, was off in his final year at college. He was attending (with my encouragement) Northwestern. Gordon and his older brother, David, grew up ingrained in *The Herald*, doing everything from delivering papers to working in our print room loading ink and cleaning the presses.

Amy's company succeeded in every way she could imagine. She continued to call me periodically, always excited, to update me on her genesis, BrandCorp. Brandcorp, as the name gives hint, specialized in one thing and that was establishing a brand for a new company or re-branding an existing company. It was the perfect business for her and no one could be more prepared to launch and lead it. Branding was like breathing to Amy.

I was fortunate being insulated by Emmit, someone who I knew I could call on for wisdom anytime. But a couple years after Amy left, when we showed we could seamlessly move on and grow, I think he was confident that his job was done. He confided in me that he wished to make his shares of the company available for a new cast of investors. His return on investment, I don't even think he could have even imagined when we first started making this dream a reality. It neared a king's ransom at the time of his departure.

We had grown exponentially from year five until the time of his departure (and, for that matter, almost every year since then). We owned more than 50 newspapers throughout the Midwest and had just begun to consider acquisitions of some small radio stations as well as regional niche magazines.

BUILD TO SELL

What I later learned was that Emmit almost always had a price where he would sell his companies, confiding in me "every entrepreneur would be wise to pick a sale price, even if it is just an ambitious price that is lofty enough to motivate you to grow the company. But always put a price in your mind for what you would like to sell your ambition and risk for well before you ever get an offer."

As it turned out, this would be one of our final lessons, one that I would allow to just marinate in my brain.

"You build the company from day one with the idea of selling it. This forces you to do all the little things right. Too many business owners don't pay themselves on the books, somehow thinking they are getting over on the tax man," he said, referring to avoiding personal and business taxes, trying to run a cash business. "This is a fool's game of hide-and-seek with the profits, which often results in multiple sets of accounting records. What they fail to realize is the only person they hurt is themselves because you can't put a value on a business like that."

When he summarized his point, he used his pause, speak lower and pause again technique to perfection. By this point, I recognized it immediately and smiled as I settled in to absorb my lesson.

"I learned from Red," he shared in a tone of reverence. It was a name from the past that always garnered my attention. Emmit shared the point in the same cadence Red would have used. "You build companies so you can sell them. This allows them to be an asset in your personal financial portfolio."

Red, even more so than Emmit, was a disciple of the fact that entrepreneurship was every person's privilege in our country—no matter their education or current lot in life—to build personal wealth. I was certain the depression, which Red experienced in a first-hand way, galvanized his respect for a dollar and the peace of mind a treasure chest of them could provide.

CONTRIBUTION

I thought, and deep down hoped, Emmit would always be sitting directly across from me at every quarterly meeting of our investors. He was like a rudder on a ship that I was lucky to have captained. Passing 70 a few years prior, I'm sure he sold when he did—not waiting for an even larger return on his initial investment—because he had a sales date and price predetermined years earlier.

In our final meeting, wrapping up his departure, I learned that he hoped to have his lifetime of ambition, persistence, involving others in his ventures and the rewards those partnerships created perpetuate good well beyond his lifetime. I think this was the other reason he sold when he did. He wanted to personally see some of that good in his life and experience it with Jenny.

With the sale of his final holdings in Midwest Media Corporation, our name at the time, he and Jenny purchased a large tract of land that would be turned into a summer camp and winter retreat center for children who were blind or had pronounced visual limitations. It was a cause that had always been close to their heart as Jenny's youngest brother was blind and so they knew first-hand the challenges this handicap brings.

FOR PROFIT OR NON-PROFIT MAKES NO DIFFERENCE

Emmit never stopped being an entrepreneur as this charitable venture fed his passion to birth a new organization that provided value to someone. Whether it was for profit or not did not matter. Keeping up to date with his progress at the camp, I learned that the pillars are the same no matter the venture. It showed because what he accomplished in his final chapter may have surpassed anything he helped build prior. If you had asked him, he wouldn't have hesitated to say it did.

He and Jenny sought to create a place where children with visual handicaps could play and participate in all the fun and games that their peers were able to enjoy in an environment where the workers had the patience and the training to encourage and facilitate them. This unique facility would be the model for others to follow and the Lake's generous gift endowed the camp and its mission well beyond their living years.

This ending personified Emmit's core value that a life well lived had contribution in its fabric. I had been educated on the value of contribution and its impact well before our partnership began. The platform was usually dinners with our wives, where his core values were truly displayed and I experienced the revelation that he was a driven but well-balanced man.

The old sage educated Christine and me with one of his most fundamental axioms, one that applied far beyond the business world.

"All of us should feel drawn to some cause that breaks our focus on self. Because of this consciousness, we are induced to use our resources—whether that be time, influence, resources, talent, or money or all of it—to make a difference."

He punctuated this axiom like he did with so many lessons. "When it is all said and done, was the world better because you were in it?"

That elementary question planted a new seed in me, and although I am ashamed to admit it, that seed has sat dormant for too long in my life.

Chapter 18

DREAM BIG

I would see in our newspaper's business section every day the New York Stock Exchange, with its listing of companies identified by their ticker symbol and their share price. This list embedded itself in my mind and my imagination teased me with the possibility well before my dream had a chance of being reality. My imagination over time convinced me to set this dream as a goal. Once it both captured my imagination and my day-to-day conscience, I knew the next step would be to strategize how to bring it to reality.

I chronicled thoughts and progress on this dream in my daily journal, a habit Red taught Emmit. He, in turn, distilled this daily discipline to me. My spiral notebook contained a cutout section of the New York Stock Exchange listings and had what I thought our ticker symbol might be, typed and taped on the newsprint, as if we were listed in that day's business section.

I viewed it daily as I not only had it in my journal, but also kept a laminated copy in my office under the glass protecting my desk and finally one on my bathroom mirror, a constant nuisance to Christine. These visual reminders drove me to not only make grand plans, but to take action. To be specific, strategic action to make this goal a reality, within a five-year period. It was when I gave myself this deadline that I became convinced my grand dream would become reality.

The deadline forced immediate actions like expanding my team as well as my cabinet. We engaged the service of GCN Investment Group, a top New York investment banking firm who specialized in bringing companies to this pinnacle, to lay the laborious ground work that would take years before we could offer our company to the public.

Along with expanding my cabinet, expanding our company's footprint was the action we needed to show our scalability; that we would soon touch all corners of the U.S. market and, in time, beyond.

I am glad Emmit saw his dream become reality, but I secretly hoped he would have held off a touch longer. Not for me, but because I knew our once local single-location newspaper would soon become a giant, affirmed by becoming a publicly held company traded on the New York Stock Exchange. Somehow, I thought this would be the crowning jewel for any entrepreneur; that this single accomplishment confirmed business success.

What made Emmit unique and so fulfilled was that he had his own definition of success and what his personal dream looked like. In that, I am certain he achieved it all.

Chapter 19

THE FINAL PILLAR

The Seven Pillars handed down to me by Emmit prepared and enabled me to provide the strategic leadership our company needed, but I learned something more following Emmit's departure that I have concluded is my one foundational pillar to stand with the seven. This **Eighth Pillar** that allowed us to not only survive startup but also experience decades of continual growth until we became the giant was *change*.

Change may come in many forms as a startup. It may be discovering new profit streams as we did with our inserts, implanting them in our newspapers even though they were never a listed item on our active business plan. Although, I learned to think of it as another reason the business plan is called active to begin with. It allowed for flexibility so modifications could be made as needed.

Change can be as simple as a course correction or something as dramatic as a complete transformation regardless of the extreme change. Willingness to change is a precept that the entrepreneur needs as a lifelong discipline.

During his life, Emmit saw stalwart companies thrive for near a generation with names known and revered the world over, but I would sadly see these same companies fall from greatness in my lifetime. The culprit was always failure to change, and they did not change because they were the giant. The giants foolishly believed they did not have to change, and it was that arrogance and void of humility that also made change impossible. On the rare occasion a giant gave in to the idea of change, it was too often too late with a reluctant buy in, which meant failure was still imminent.

Over time, the landscape changed. The world began to move at a considerably greater speed with innovations being launched instantaneously to the world. To survive, you had to at the very least adapt, often evolve and sometimes transmute your identity because a competitor could arise so fast and so formidable in this new age that your company's existence was always at risk.

THE HUMBLE GIANT

The humble giant never considered its place at the head of the table permanent. No, it knew this place needed to be earned every day by being hyper alert to any innovation that could allow their present business to be offered faster, cheaper or better to its customers.

With this lesson, my leadership fostered a culture where ideas were embraced, analyzed, rewarded and finally implemented. This was my contribution and I believe it fostered a culture where everyone on the team, no matter his or her position, was encouraged to contribute ideas. I am certain our team members were our greatest resource in our effort to continually innovate and thrive.

We understood the need for progress, expanding our core business to include multiple forms of media as well as content partners that had fresh and different platforms to assist in our goal of providing valuable advertising vehicles within media to our clients.

The accomplishment of this goal and the continual movement towards our vision confirmed to me what our next leader most required.

Chapter 20

THE DECISION

M y enormous oak desk—a gift from the board when we became a public company—became the focal point of an office that Emmit would have scoffed at, I am sure. Truth be told, it's not my style either, but it has served well as a focal point to discuss deals we closed over the last decade, which positioned us to grow an already formidable company in the media industry. Our two largest hinges are now cable TV and satellite media with our recent acquisition of U.S. Satellite, while we are still implanted in more than 50 cities with print newspapers that are also leaders in local mobile content that can be viewed on people's phones.

Sitting there at my desk, I was reflecting on how I missed Emmit's laugh and, most of all, his wisdom. The simple way he could give an answer, but not tell you it was the answer to take. He had a way of sharing insights that I was so fortunate and privileged to experience. I don't think I will ever stop missing that.

Thinking about him leads me to withdraw from under the glass top of my desk a notecard I placed there when the behemoth was first set in place. It is the very same notecard I had watched Emmit putting away before our very first lunch meetings at Sara's Diner and so many times after.

He finally relented, sharing its content with me at one of our last meetings. There was a time I viewed it more frequently, but that was when my desk—and my responsibilities—were a fraction of this size. Now I must use it to jar my various thoughts about our business's past and its future to a conclusion.

The card has yellowed some and the ink is faded, but still legible. It reads:

Today, I am grateful to be a very successful entrepreneur, which allows me to give generously, and this is because I have surrounded myself with a team I trust that shares my vision. I will seek to listen, involve, promote and partner with them and never take their ideas, talent, time, energy and loyalty for granted.

Reading it again jolts me, reminding me of the team that helped build that which I'm now about to pass on.

Looking at my watch I realize it is seven days almost to the hour since I walked Charlie Calloway from my office promising a recommendation soon, although I made no promise of the direction I would endorse. Somehow, I do not think Charlie has experienced a great deal of disappointment in his life. My guess is that he has been hired for every position he has ever sought. I never sensed in my time with him that he was hungry for success. No, he expects success to just be there for him. I know success has to be earned daily by a company and it cannot be assumed that just existing will be enough.

The decision has become clearer to me over the last week, with someone unexpected rising up in my mind. Have I taken his broad contribution for granted? I ask myself this over and over, demanding my conscience to answer. The board had been adamant about a big hire since the public debacle with David Emerson and I recognized my verdict would be a stark contrast.

THE BETRAYAL

Why a grand hire, I've asked myself. Over the past weeks, I've pondered over what qualities constitute this level of a leader. In our case and specifically to our board, the answer is someone with experience leading a large division or company in media who has a pedigree and personality that satiates Wall Street's appetite. That is why everyone touted our acquisition of U.S. Satellite. It not only brought us a needed platform, but when completed would also procure its dynamic leader.

That would be the charismatic boy wonder David Emerson, who started the business from his parents' basement during his sophomore summer break from Harvard. Like Bill Gates, he never returned. It is his story, so parallel to Gates's, that made People Magazine name him one of America's most fascinating people under 40.

But at the midnight hour of our acquisition, which was chronicled more as a merger cementing old media with new, their brash young trailblazer requested a sabbatical, declaring he was suffering from burnout, confessing in a much viewed interview that he had never taken more than a day off since starting his business.

Burnout for some reason—if you ask me he had a pollster test it—was accepted with little skepticism. To get support and even admiration for his departure, he would focus a short season on humanitarian interests. David was always aware of his image but the humanitarian part, I never bought into.

The betrayal came six months and one sunrise after the acquisition was complete. The boy wonder, knowing he had met a contract requirement—one the board, who handled the final contract, never completely made me aware of, and an omission I can only excuse because they genuinely never assumed he would pursue it—was now free to start or to partner in a new venture. He had enough capital with the sale of U.S. Satellite to harness an army, and the business he has started in time will transplant itself into media and be a giant that MW Media one day will need to slay.

When I found out what they had done, I dismantled their logic behind closed doors. The inclusion of a muddy non-compete clause in his contract had language that to this day confuses me and, I am convinced, must have been drafted in the final hours with no one taking great notice of its clever use of terms of titles that could bring great relief to its soon-to-be leader.

I question whether he ever planned to lead our company knowing his void would, in fact, leave the giant vulnerable and this I shared. I protested from the beginning against their rush to bring David Emerson to the throne without heeding my warning for a time of adjustment and accountability. The board, now humbled and disarmed, made it clear that they would endorse my recommendation but this sole responsibility—a responsibility I never planned to make on my own—I am now forced to render and to render soon.

THE RIGHT HIRE

In retrospect, I conclude there are two qualities that have allowed us to succeed over the near 35 years I have led this company. First, we revere ideas, knowing they are the seed of profit as well as survival. Without them, there was no chance of ever becoming a giant. So I've concluded that the next shepherd will need to embrace a culture where ideas, after careful analysis, will flow unimpeded to implementation. This can only exist where there is truly an attitude of humility from its highest-level management. The second quality, humility, creates the setting that keeps everyone from becoming complacent. It is the mindset that is able to recognize change as a requirement of success, not an admission of failure.

I concluded, we do not need a big hire, we need the right hire. This decision is now quite obvious to me because I am sure the two qualities that must continue at MW Media will do so under his stewardship.

We all ask and often pray for a sign when making a decision, but often fail to then look for that hint of an answer. But when a serendipitous moment took place earlier this evening as I left my office, it jarred my consciousness. It was the moment that cemented my decision. The event was quite routine, but I guess I had grown callous to it, but seeing it again provided the confirmation I needed.

Our executive staff parking is located under the building we reside in, directly off an elevator reserved for upper level management. It allows those in high positions to get in and get out without delay or distraction, an expressway of sorts. I admit, I've used and loved this perk for years, but I asked myself rhetorically, this moment, knowing the answer. Why had I never once in 11 years in this building seen Gordon Merrick in this elevator of the chosen? I had ridden it thousands of times and had never once shared a ride with him.

What I found even more humbling, when it first came to my attention quite some time after we had moved into this glass cathedral of capitalism, was that Gordon not only passed on the elevator, but also on that prodigious parking space as well. His reasoning, as he put it, was that "it serves better as a reward for a job well done for one of my team members."

For him, it was a reward for doing something outstanding and he always found a reason to give it away to someone deserving recognition. I should have noticed it earlier, given how I would see a row of expensive automobiles congested in this chosen field of asphalt next to one older or modest car or minivan that just seemed out of place.

Remembering Gordon's humility provided the moment of clarity I demanded. Gordon was it I knew. He is the perfect choice. He has the DNA within him of what grew our company, modeled to him since childhood simply by growing up in Amy's house. Thinking back, I can remember Gordon and his brother David both working cleaning our presses, to both having paper routes delivering *The Herald,* well before even high school. Gordon would, after graduating from Northwestern and marrying his high school sweetheart, come on board full-time assisting with operations under Martin.

Martin retired within a few years, convinced at the time that Gordon could lead the operations division. To be forthright, at the time I was not so convinced because Gordon was not as detailed as Martin, but I learned quickly he knew how to delegate, motivate and brought other valuable skills that allowed him to serve in a broad capacity over the years

I am not sure what position within the company he has not held at some point. The names of the people Gordon had worked for or with all bring back fond reflections, reminding me of those who participated in our initial survival.

Gordon currently is an executive vice president leading cable advertising, our largest source of revenue. He has done anything he has been asked to do, but I cannot remember him ever demanding to do anything specific. This, I am convinced, is not due to lack of ambition, but because with our incredible growth there was always a vital position that needed to be manned and he was always quick to absorb the overflow. He had great "capacity" a trait I came to appreciate over the years. Maybe I took his likeability and broad skill set for granted because he was never one who jockeyed for a promotion, something I had grown accustomed to seeing in recent years by others.

THE CALL

Realizing my verdict is final, I request Linda to put in a call to see if she can get Jake Worthingon on the phone. I do not want to drag this call or any further deliberations into another weekend. Christine has been patient; she was always so patient. Linda tells me Mr. Worthington is on my Line 1, and with that I levy my decision and begin to explain to Jake how I think it will work.

"Jake, I want to first apologize for taking so long, but as you can imagine this is not just any team member we are adding."

Jake, barely letting me finish my introduction, bursts in like a child at Christmas. "Is Charlie our guy?"

"He could be," I respond, knowing the board will have to confirm my selection to make it official, "but, Jake, I think I have overlooked someone who is already in the building. I am certain he could make this work as well as we've all hoped for. In the end, it may even make this recent debacle our good fortune because it gave us time to cement the right appointee to my position. We may want to add one or two board members, but it is my hope that may not even be necessary since Jeb Brady and Dillon Henrik's terms are over shortly and I think they may be open to expediting that."

Holding back for as long as he could—I am guessing it had already felt like an eternity, Jake blurts out, "What are you suggesting, Johnny?"

"We should ask Gordon Merrick to take my position and allow me to serve one term as co-chairman of the board. I know after this last year, you need a break."

I can hear him sigh and hope it's a sigh of agreement.

"This would keep New York happy," I add, referring to our stock valuation, "and allow either Malcolm Gilstone or, even better, Sherry Trisdale to agree to serve on the board. I am convinced they were the ones doing the heavy lifting for Emerson. Both are very smart people we still have under contract for consulting after the acquisition. This would be smart, strategic and allow us to make a peace offering to their team. And we'd maintain the culture we have in this building, which I don't think should be taken for granted."

I sense Jake's wheels turning, I just have to close the sale. Like I learned so many years ago, I don't need to overwhelm him with reasons. I just need to help him understand the value of what I was offering.

"Jake, it gives us the best of what we have and the best of our newest partner. They understand the global landscape as well as anybody. In time, we will need to appoint an executive VP to focus on our global market, but for now this I believe is the appropriate answer."

I hear Jake take a deep breath, but he pauses for a moment. It's not like Jake Worthington to ever be at a loss for words, but this time I wait. I give him time to see the value of this deal on his own.

"Well, I have to tell you, Johnny, I like it. I'm sure the board will as well, but why the change of heart? We asked you last time if you'd join the board, but you seemed quite hesitant."

"I always liked Gordon and, for that matter, his whole family. Besides, you know Emerson was never going to approve of the old guy giving him advice and Charlie would have put on that smile for me, but he wouldn't have been much different."

But what I trusted most and did not share with Jake is that I believe Gordon will most certainly steward the Eight Pillars and in time add one of his own.

Want To Learn More?

Are you looking for personal business startup coaching?
Need help determining whether you or your business idea is a
good fit for the entrepreneurial journey?
Do you have a passion for owning your own business?
VISIT US AT
www.seancastrina.com

About the Author

Sean C. Castrina is a serial entrepreneur, business coach and sought after speaker. He has started more than 15 successful companies over 20 years and this portfolio continues to grow. His companies have ranged from retail, direct mail marketing and advertising to real estate development and home services. He is the author of the bestselling startup book *The 8 Unbreakable Rules for Business Start-Up Success*, which was the most endorsed startup book ever written at the time of release and hailed by countless *New York Times* Bestselling authors and business giants.

Acknowledgements

There is no one who encourages or sustains my dreams more than my wife Bev, who in her steady way just keeps me going forward. So, my dear, I love and thank you most for the decades of supporting all my crazy ventures including the idea to write books and share what I have learned to help others achieve their dreams.

To Collin and Baylee, my children, who listen to my countless ideas for new businesses, books and chapters that I think others will value. And to all my business partners, and employees, over the years who I have learned so much from. And finally to two of the best editors I could ask for, my mom who always finds a word that could be changed, and finally Ben Foster, my lunch partner, who along with teaching me endless business lessons has added great improvements to this manuscript, thank you.

CPSIA information can be obtained at www.ICGtesting.com
Printed in the USA
BVOW04s0859131015

421941BV00026B/43/P